AMERICAN MASTERS
Sculpture from Brookgreen Gardens

ROBIN R. SALMON
with contributions by
Ilene Susan Fort and Lauretta Dimmick

BROOKGREEN
Gardens

Traveling Exhibition Schedule

June 12-August 16, 1998
    Jack S. Blanton Museum of Art
    University of Texas, Austin, Texas

January 16-April 18, 1999
    The Terra Museum of American Art, Chicago, Illinois

May 10-July 30, 1999
    The National Sculpture Society, New York City

September 5-October 31, 1999
    Tampa Museum of Art, Tampa, Florida

American Masters: Sculpture from Brookgreen Gardens

The American Masters Exhibit has been made possible by a generous grant from BMW with additional funding provided by the Henry Luce Foundation.

This exhibition was designed by Staples & Charles Ltd. and fabricated by Exhibits Unlimited, both of Alexandria, Virginia.

Published by: Brookgreen Gardens, Pawleys Island, South Carolina

ISBN 0-9638206-3-X

Catalogue designed by Lesnik Himmelsbach Wilson Hearl and Hirsch, Inc., Myrtle Beach, South Carolina. Photography by Reggie Williams, Charlotte, North Carolina. Printing by State Printing Company, Columbia, South Carolina.

Front cover: *Resting Stag* by Elie Nadelman (1882-1946), bronze, c. 1939, 16.5 x 21 x 8 in. (41.9 x 53.3 20.3 cm).

Frontispiece: *Evening* by Paul Manship (1885-1966), bronze, c. 1917, 44 x 67 x 12 in. (111.8 x 169.2 x 30.5 cm). *Shown at Brookgreen Gardens only.*

Back cover: View of Brookgreen Gardens with *Boy and Squirrel* by Walker Hancock (b. 1901), Batesville marble, 1928, 38 x 38 x 19 in. (96.5 x 96.5 x 48.2 cm.).

Contents

Introduction

by Robin R. Salmon

The Fountain of the Muses by Carl Milles (1875-1955), bronze, 1949-1955, life-size figures, fifteen piece fountain group.

Sculpture as a fine art is a relatively young concept in America. Although utilitarian sculpture such as ship figureheads and carved signs were created from the time of the nation's infancy, the idea of three-dimensional art having a less functional purposes did not arise until the early nineteenth century. Once the idea developed, artists began creating works for our nation's monuments, gardens, private estates and individual patrons. The neoclassical sculptors of the mid-nineteenth century adhered to the principles of classicism, yet they utilized subject matter that was uniquely American. The rise of naturalism in sculpture involved the accurate presentation of a subject, including the pose, costume and surface texture. These figures gradually took on increased significance, both in scale and complexity of composition, heralding the beginning of heroic realism and the integration of sculpture and architecture.

This activity reached its zenith in the late nineteenth century with the advent of the Gilded Age at the height of American industrialism. Expositions around the turn of the century, beginning with the World's Columbian

Exposition at Chicago in 1893, promoted the City Beautiful movement, a return to the principles of classicism in building and landscape design. The need for sculptural ornamentation, fountains and focal points lent itself readily to the movement and fostered a new generation of sculptors working in collaboration with architects and landscape designers. The spate of millionaires created by rapid technological innovations and the rise of American financial empires produced opportunities for these artists to ornament country retreats and city mansions in accordance with the owners' economic status. This wealth also allowed sculptors and architects to reflect the material glory of a prosperous nation through grand public monuments and buildings commemorating benefactors and heroes.

European art schools, such as the École des Beaux-Arts at Paris, provided the training for practitioners of the beaux-arts style during the American Renaissance from 1876 to 1915. The evolution from Beaux-Arts to Academicism occurred in a smooth transition at the turn of the century. Proponents of Academicism held the same beliefs as the Beaux-Arts artists, however, they worked on a smaller scale, emphasizing beautiful and genteel subjects. This shift in emphasis brought about more personal themes such as the innocence of childhood and the joys of motherhood which appealed to a wider audience. At the same time, romanticized images of the American West were being recorded in sculpture of animals, Indians and cowboys.

Beginning in 1930, with the acquisition of four once splendid rice plantations on the South Carolina coast, Archer M. Huntington and his wife, Anna Hyatt Huntington, undertook to build the first public sculpture garden in America and one of the largest and most significant collections of sculpture.

Archer Huntington was an industrialist, heir to a railroad and shipping fortune, who used his wealth in a manner that set new standards for philanthropy. The founder of several museums and an avid collector of objects, ranging from antiquities to contemporary American art, Huntington provided assistance to artists by sponsoring major exhibitions under the auspices of the National Sculpture Society. Personally interested in poetry and literature, Huntington supported scholarly pursuits and endowed the chair of poetry at the Library of Congress. He was himself a respected academician, and actively involved with the American Numismatic Society, the American Academy of Arts and Letters, the National Academy of Design and the Hispanic Society of America. Anna Hyatt Huntington, a renowned sculptor, continued to create the monuments and animal figures for which she was acclaimed, even after her marriage at the age of forty-seven to Huntington, one of the wealthiest men in America. This union of kindred spirits fostered a beneficence that reached scores of museums, arts organizations and institutions of higher learning around the world.

The Huntington's intentions for what became known as Brookgreen Gardens, a 350-acre public sculpture garden set within a 9,000 acre tract, were well defined from the outset. They did not collect purely for their own pleasure, as did other members of wealthy society. From the beginning, they determined their collection would be available to the public. It would include only figurative works by American sculptors that could be effectively exhibited out-of-doors in the gardens Anna Huntington was designing for the grounds of Brookgreen.

Through their lifetimes, the Huntingtons added to the collection and expanded the display. Archer Huntington proclaimed it "a quiet joining of hands between science and art" that had as its object the presentation of the natural life of a given district as a museum. Huntington added, "as it is a garden, and gardens have from early times been rightly embellished by the art of the sculptor, that principle has found expression in American creative art...At first the garden was intended to contain the sculpture of Anna Hyatt Huntington. This has gradually found extension in an outline collection representative of the history of American sculpture, from

Persephone by Marshall Maynard Fredericks, bronze, 52.5 x 30 x 30 in. (133.3 x 76.2 x 76.2 cm.) *Shown in the traveling exhibition only.*

the nineteenth century, which finds its natural setting out of doors."

After their deaths (Archer Huntington in 1955 and Anna Hyatt Huntington in 1973), the Board of Trustees of Brookgreen Gardens continued to expand the collection while adhering to the founders' focus on figurative works by American sculptors. The result of this sixty-six-year tradition is the largest collection of its type anywhere, some 580 works, representing virtually every major American sculptor. Brookgreen Gardens is today a National Historic Landmark.

Throughout the years, none of the works within the Brookgreen collection had ever left its setting within the gardens. Moreover, until last year, the by-laws of the institution prohibited the removal of any piece for loan to another museum. New leadership within the board and staff realized that the time was at hand to enhance the exhibition methods on site for this singular and extraordinary collection, and to make it available to a national audience. Thus the planning began for the first temporary exhibition in the institution's history: "American Masters: Sculpture from Brookgreen Gardens." Forty-two of the most important works in the collection were gathered from their traditional garden settings and placed into the newly renovated, state-of-the-art galleries of the Callie and John Rainey Sculpture Pavilion.

The 175-year-period covered by "American Masters: Sculpture from Brookgreen Gardens" includes objects by the foremost sculptors in American history. Achievement is the core of the exhibition. The exhibition presents not only the work of those artists who are considered masters, but sculptures that are their masterworks. Each sculpture presents elements of the genius of its creator: artistic concerns, inspiration or the ways in which cultural, social and political influences of the time were depicted.

Aside from presenting obvious achievement in sculpture, the works chosen for the exhibition reflect the artists' personalities and preferences. The tiny *Head of Nero* by Gutzon Borglum seems an unlikely choice to represent the sculptor best known for his colossal works at Mount Rushmore. Nevertheless, Borglum considered this sculpture to be his masterpiece: "There was something in me at the time that allowed me to create my Nero."

Horatio Greenough is represented by his earliest known attempt at stone-carving. The small head of *Bacchus,* with its enigmatic smile, was believed lost for most of its 175-year existence. Created when he was fourteen, it was given by Greenough to his Harvard classmate, Paul Trapier of South Carolina, and remained in private hands until it was acquired for Brookgreen Gardens in 1994. This exhibition marks the first time it has ever been publicly displayed. Since it was Greenough's first work in stone, *Bacchus* has a larger significance as one of the earliest examples of American sculpture, by virtue of Greenough's status as America's first professional sculptor.

The exhibition also includes recent works by two of today's most accomplished sculptors of the human figure — *Basket Dancer* by Glenna Goodacre and *Wind on the Water* by Richard McDermott Miller. This huge female figure with billowing drapery is poised on one foot, arms lifted above her head, as she takes a giant step forward into the wind. Due to its size, Miller's sculpture is shown as a photographic mural in the traveling exhibition. Goodacre's depiction of a costumed participant in a Pueblo woman's ritual dance epitomizes her modeling skill and sense of composition. Other contemporary artists in the exhibition, Isidore Margulies, Charles Parks, and Marshall Fredericks, have works in bronze created in the 1970s and 1980s. Parks' *Long Long Thoughts* provides a charming depiction of childhood inspired by the poetry of Longfellow. Fredericks' *Persephone* and Margulies' *Debbie II* present the female figure in diametrically opposed interpretations—fantasy versus super realism. *The Windy Doorstep* by Abastenia Eberle, *Maidenhood* by George Grey Barnard, *Communion* by Brenda Putnam and *The Duchess* by Henry Clews, Jr., employ genre, realism and caricature in depicting four vastly different images of women. Eberle, Barnard and Clews all strived to create works that presented social and political messages within the context of their times.

Works in bronze such as *The Sun Vow* by Hermon MacNeil and *The Bronco Buster* by Frederic Remington are deemed important contributions within the *oeuvre* of these individual sculptors. Anna Hyatt Huntington's *Joan of Arc* not only made her reputation as a sculptor of note, but also attained historical eminence as the first equestrian monument of a woman by a woman, and as the first monument that depicted Joan with authentic arms and armor.

Fountain sculpture is represented by the work of two incomparable sculptors within that field. Janet Scudder, with her delightful bronze *Frog Baby,* was known for joyous figures of children in the Italian Renaissance tradition. Carl Milles made his mark as the greatest twentieth century sculptor of fountains with groups such as *The Fountain of the Muses.*

The field of animal sculpture includes *Penguins* by Albert Laessle, *Saluki* by Gertrude Lathrop, *Greyhounds Unleashed* by Katharine Lane Weems and *Tête-à-Tête* by Charlotte Dunwiddie. Each of these sculptors carved a singular niche within that genre. The common thread among these works is the artist's ability to endow their sculpture with certain characteristics of each animal. Thus, Laessle, Lathrop, Weems and Dunwiddie became known for their innate sense of animal personality, in addition to their knowledge of anatomy and features.

American figurative sculpture is experiencing a renewed public and scholarly interest. "American Masters: Sculpture from Brookgreen Gardens" responds to this interest with this selection of pioneer artists and landmark works ranging from 1819 to the present.

The New Symbolism

by Ilene Susan Fort

Lorado Taft (1860-1936) and his model for the *Fountain of Creation*, 1910, which included the figure, *Daughter of Pyrrah.* Courtesy of Chicago Historical Society, DH-055835; photographer: *Chicago Daily News.*

At the turn of the century, a number of American sculptors were hailed as dreamers, lauded for their creativity in inventing imaginative work of a new order. Metaphysical in nature, the art of George Grey Barnard, Charles Grafly, Lorado Taft and others explored the human condition.

Their art appeared during a period of cultural crisis. The nation was experiencing numerous and often contradictory transformations in response to growing industrialization, urbanization, secularization and immigration. Although nineteenth-century positivism and technological rationalization had encouraged the idea of progress, overcivilization undermined confidence. Some, sensing the loss of a religious foundation, searched elsewhere for authentic experiences of an emotional or spiritual significance.[1] The "New Symbolism" of Barnard and his colleagues was in response to this situation.[2] As William Howe Downes explained, their art went "to the very heart of the life of men and women" of their day, and it was "the sheer humanity of...[such] creations which...gave a fresh realization of the divinity of human nature, its boundless possibilities, and its glorious destiny."

American imaginative sculptors probed the communal psychic through the human figure. The body for them was not so much an ideal form to be extolled, as in Neoclassicism, but an expression of human emotions. Through pose, gesture and the degree of naturalism, a figure could convey a range of experiences, from the most personal dreams of the artist to universal situations. And it was the French aesthetics of Symbolism that encouraged the Americans to reject traditional allegory and look inward for a more truthful emotive art form.

Symbolism emerged in the 1880s as a reaction against the materialism of the era. Symbolist writers and artists, such as the poet Stephane Mallarmé, rejected the visible world, considering superficial details inconsequential, preferring to explore beneath outward surfaces to discover deeper truths within. Auguste Rodin was the most famous sculptor to exemplify the late romantic philosophy of Symbolism. Beginning in the 1880s with *The Gates of Hell,* he examined the unconscious and private world of people by focusing on such themes as dreams,

Augustus Saint-Gaudens (1848-1907), third from left, and helpers at his Cornish, New Hampshire, studio posed with plaster statue of the Sherman Monument, c. 1892. Courtesy of U. S. Department of the Interior, National Parks Service, Saint-Gaudens National Historic Site, Cornish, New Hampshire.

earlier through illustrations and articles.[4] Publications on Rodin and his art were extensive, beginning as early as 1889 with the landmark series of articles by the American sculptor Truman H. Bartlett.[5]

The influence of Rodin on American sculpture was overwhelming.[6] Yet even before the 1890s, when he became a cult figure, hints of a more subjective strain appeared within the parameters of American neoclassical and academic sculpture. The endless repetition of harmonious, ideal nudes exemplifying great virtues and realistic portraits and war memorials had become sterile. A new spirit was inaugurated by Augustus Saint-Gaudens. Although his *Puritan* began as a commemorative monument honoring Samuel Chapin, founder of Springfield, Massachusetts, it signified much more. The colonial deacon's erect posture and forward stride evokes his religious zeal. For a later reworking, Saint-Gaudens departed from his original faithful delineation to create "an embodiment...of the 'Puritan,'" elongating Chapin's face into a stern New England visage.[7] By transforming the portrait of a specific person into an emblem of morality and duty, the sculptor conveyed the human spirit behind the deeds.

Saint-Gaudens was frequently compared to Rodin, his contemporary. Each emerged as an artist of significance in the late 1870s and created his most imaginative and enduring compositions during the next two decades. Saint-Gaudens's knowledge of Rodin dated from the 1876 Centennial Exhibition held in Philadelphia; by 1887 he ranked Rodin one of France's most important sculptors and a significant influence on his own art.[8]

Later Saint-Gaudens numbered among the many who considered Rodin bizarre and offensive in his use of extreme emotionalism and departure from accepted standards of beauty.[9] The critic William Brownell differed in his opinion, understanding that Rodin regarded all aspects of nature as beautiful, his visionary imagination transforming even the seemingly ugly into something lofty.[10] Rodin's *Balzac,* grand in its erect stature and exalted spirit, initially caused controversy because it was thought to lack grace. Lorado Taft and Gutzon Borglum realized the statue was one of Rodin's finest, an excellent example of his potent naturalism. It even encouraged the expressive handling of Borglum's *Nero.* According to Symbolist philosophy, the mind is the center of a person's intellect and soul. The heads of both *Balzac* and *Nero* are craggy, glyptic forms modeled with deep recessions to create strong shadows. But *Nero* is no intelligent emperor a citizen should admire, but rather his fleshy, sagging face and terrifying, deep wide eyes indicate the madness that would culminate in his suicide after a life of murder.

Specific historic personalities did not exemplify the typical subject matter of American imaginative sculptors. Pre-modern themes and those of an eternal character with no time reference were sought. Usually the figure was nude, a generic any and every man, the bearer of

the human mind, sexuality and sin. He shared the Symbolist anti-rational stance, striving to create an art of suggestion, rather than description. While still retaining references to reality, Rodin created a world of shadows and ambiguity. As the American critic Royal Cortissoz explained, Rodin "brings from behind the veil the very soul of war, of love, or misery, or joy."[3]

There were many parallels and connections between European Symbolism and American imaginative art. Beginning in the 1880s, Americans became familiar with Symbolist literature through translations and commentaries. Boston intellectual circles, at the heart of the New England imaginative literary tradition, were particularly enthusiastic. Although European Symbolist paintings did not appear in significant numbers until the 1913 New York Armory Show, the art of Paul Gauguin, Gustave Moreau, Odilon Redon and others was known much life's experiences. The frailty of humanity thus became the source of many turn-of-the-century sculptures, as demonstrated by Paul Wayland Bartlett's *Study in Bronze*. Inspired by Rodin's *The Thinker*, the most famous motif from *The Gates* composition, Bartlett sensitively modeled a figure huddled in despair, seemingly defeated despite his strong body. The theme of a crouched or seated figure, contemplating his life or resting from his toils, would become popular with American sculptors.

Barnard and Taft shared with Rodin the ambition to create complicated, multi-figured projects, such as *The Gates*, on metaphysical themes. The destiny of humanity, represented by the life span of one person or the ages of mankind, was a frequent theme. Sounding like a mystic, Barnard explained that people had suffered enough in ignorance and darkness and the time had come to search for true knowledge by whatever means available, including art.[11] Barnard carved *Maidenhood* shortly after completing *The Hewer*, a heroic figure that was to be the first of an ensemble on primitive man.

American sculptors experienced difficulties in completing elaborate schemes just as Rodin had with *The Gates*: Barnard left unfinished his *Rainbow Arch* and Taft *The Fountain of Creation*. Taft explored imaginative works as early as the 1890s, but increasingly emphasized symbolic content during the following two decades. His *Daughter of Pyrrha* was created for *The Fountain of Creation*, intended as a pendant to *The Fountain of Time* (Washington Park, Chicago). According to Greek legend, Deucalion and Pyrrha were the parents of the human race, created from rocks, after the flood. Taft arranged the figurative groupings of *The Fountain of Creation* in a ring to reveal the sequence of mankind's physical evolution: first shapeless beings emerging from stones, then newly formed figures on their knees and finally fully developed, erect persons. Hands to her head, one of Pyrrha's daughters is just becoming conscious of her existence. The idea of a person awakening to various states of being—life in general, sexuality, spirituality—was a constant theme of Symbolists and one adopted enthusiastically by Americans.

Charles Grafly created perhaps the most enigmatic sculptures. Even though their meaning was incomprehensible to many, his symbolic sculptures attracted considerable attention. Taft wrote of Grafly's *The Symbol of Life* (1897), now in the collection of the Pennsylvania Academy of the Fine Arts, Philadelphia, "I could not fathom its meaning very readily," but went on to praise it.[12] *Vulture of War* was originally conceived as part of an ensemble of four figures about war, but was the only one completed. The personification is a scavenger in the process of gathering war's carnage. His face is brutal and his body menacing in its physical strength. Bending and slightly off balance, his pose heightens the psychological tension, making the figure even more threatening.[13] Grafly chose not to depict Mars, the traditional personification of war, nor a soldier, thereby rejecting contemporary belief in the heroism of battle. His sculpture deals with the reality of war.

American Symbolism was generally more positive and life affirming than European manifestations. Rodin relished exploring sin in *The Gates* but Americans were wary. Even Borglum found the intensity of his *Nero* disturbing years after he had modeled it. But horrific and decadent themes did appear. Henry Clews, Jr., was by far the American most fascinated with evil. Combining satire and cynicism, Clews created a bizarre vocabulary of distorted and exaggerated figures in the tradition of medieval grotesquery. Clews's *Thinker*, (1914) at Brookgreen Gardens, with its elaborate base, symbolized the institutions and attitudes that he considered to be the follies of pre-World War I: religion, socialism, materialism. Even Clews's own upper-class society was fodder for his attacks. *The Duchess* is a naked woman, her fan and string of pearls—remnants of her pretentious lifestyle—no longer able to hide her withered body and evil pride.

Rodin's belief in the emotive potential of the human figure revealed the power of sculpture as a tool for self expression. And the "New Symbolism" of American sculptors enabled them to turn inward, delving into their own psyches as well as the soul of the nation.

NOTES:
1. Lears, T. J. Jackson, *No Place of Grace: Antimodernism and the Transformation of American Culture, 1880-1920* (New York: Pantheon, 1981), 32.
2. Downes, William Howe, "Mr. Barnard's Exhibit in Boston, Which Appealed to the Connoisseurs and the Crowd Alike," *World's Work* 17 (February 1909): 11268. Although Downes was referring only to the art of Barnard, the term could easily apply to other American sculptors creating symbolic art at this time.
3. Cortissoz, Royal, "The Work of Auguste Rodin," *Current Literature* 29 (December 1900): 705.
4. Eldredge, Charles C., *American Imagination and Symbolist Painting*, (New York: Grey Art Gallery and Study Center, New York University, 1979), 18-24.
5. Bartlett, Truman H., "Auguste Rodin, Sculptor," *American Architect and Building News* 25 (January-May 1889).
6. For the most extensive examination of Rodin's impact on American sculpture, see the author's "The Cult of Rodin and the Birth of Modernism in America," in *The Figure in American Sculpture: A Question of Modernity* (Los Angeles: Los Angeles County Museum of Art, 1995): 22-53.
7. Saint-Gaudens, Homer, ed., *The Reminiscences of Augustus Saint Gaudens* (New York: Century, 1913), I: 354.
8. Merriam Dictionary questionnaire, 1887, in R. W. Gilder Collection, Manuscript Division, New York Public Library.
9. Saint-Gaudens, 1913, II: 50.
10. Brownell, W. C., "Two French Sculptors: Rodin-Dalou," *Century Illustrated Monthly* 41 (November 1890): 29.
11. Barnard quoted in Armstrong, Regina, "The Sculptor of 'Pan': Mr. George Grey Barnard and His Work," *The Critic* 33 (November 1898): 356.
12. Taft, Lorado, "Charles Grafly, Sculptor," *Brush and Pencil* 3 (March 1899): 347-8.
13. Simpson, Pamela H., "The Sculpture of Charles Grafly," Ph.D. diss., University of Delaware, 1974, p. 36.

Suffragettes, Free Spirits and Trendsetters: Women Sculptors in America

by Robin R. Salmon

Tis time my friends, we cogitate,
And make some desperate stand,
Or else our sister artists here
Will drive us from the land.

It does seem hard that we at last
Have rivals in the clay,
When for so many happy years
We had it all our way.

— Male sculptors' lament in *The Doleful Ditty of the Roman Caffe Greco* by Harriet Hosmer[1]

In the mid-nineteenth century a group of expatriate artists traveled to Rome where they studied, established studios and created the new American sculpture. Among this group were nine women, dubbed the "White

Anna Hyatt Huntington (seen working on model for *Joan of Arc*): portrait by Marion Boyd Allen, courtesy of Maier Musem of Art, Randolph-Macon Woman's College, Lynchburg, Virgina.

Marmorean Flock" by writer Henry James.[2] They were pioneers - their lifestyles and choices of career over marriage and motherhood broke new ground and made way for other women artists to follow. They were continually doing battle with male critics and sculptors. It was considered shocking that these artists used unclothed models for their sculpture. It was also beyond Victorian conventions for a woman to take responsibility for her life, choosing to live without a male provider. These women sculptors must have presented an intimidating, even frightening, picture to their colleagues and their colleagues' wives. Prominent among them were Edmonia Lewis and Harriet Hosmer.

Edmonia Lewis (c. 1844 - c. 1911) was the first American sculptor, male or female, of African and Native American ancestry. The daughter of a gentleman's servant and a Chippewa woman, Lewis spent her youth in New York State with her mother's tribe and was given the name, Wildfire. Drawing upon her dual background, she created this country's first sculpture depicting subjects inspired by a minority heritage: *Hagar* cast into the wilderness, symbolic of the black woman in white society; *Forever Free* depicting a pair of freed slaves; and *The Old Arrow Maker and his Daughter,* one of a series of groups based on Longfellow's poem, *The Song of Hiawatha.* Despite the popularity of her work in the late nineteenth century, and her importance as the first significant non-white sculptor in America, Lewis's career fell into obscurity and the exact date of her death is unknown.

Harriet Hosmer (1830 - 1908), small in stature but fiercely independent, produced a body of work that was considered outstanding by contemporary critics. Yet, she suffered from attacks against her character when her free-spirited lifestyle caused tongues to wag and against her art when she was accused in print of presenting as her own the work of male sculptors. She promptly threatened to sue for libel and the accusations were retracted. Hosmer's sculpture was often imbued with feminist symbolism—something quite extraordinary for her time. The captive queen of Palmyra, *Zenobia,* considered her masterpiece, was presented not as a defeated victim but as a strong, dignified heroine, the manacles at her wrists treated more like ornaments than objects of restraint. The subject of a play by Shelley, *Beatrice Cenci,* asleep in her cell before execution for murdering her incestuous father, was seen as a symbol of woman enduring life in a man's world. Hosmer was moved to write to Phebe Hanaford, one of the first American clergywomen:

I honor every woman who has strength enough to step out of the beaten path when she feels that her walk lies in another; strength enough to stand up and be laughed at if necessary. That is a bitter pill we must swallow at the beginning; but I regard those pills as tonics quite essential to one's mental salvation...But in a few years it will not be thought strange that women should be preachers and sculptors, and everyone who comes after us will have to bear fewer and fewer blows. Therefore I say, I honor all those who step boldly forward, and, in spite of ridicule and criticism, pave a broader way for the women of the next generation.[3]

In 1889 a group of painters and sculptors organized the Woman's Art Club of New York, forerunner of the National Association of Women Artists, in response to frustrating years of being rejected from exhibitions by all-male juries and of being barred from serving on powerful committees of art organizations. Artists depended upon their work being seen in important annual exhibitions such as those of the National Academy of Design, one of the country's oldest art organizations. Not only was the professional recognition crucial but, before the existence of commercial art galleries, exhibitions were the primary avenue to reach potential buyers. By 1911 with nearly one thousand members nationwide, the club's annual exhibition prompted an article addressing the issue of a woman's position in the art world. A critic, Christian Brinton, acknowledged that women had been historically important in the "development of taste" and cited the Woman's Building in Chicago at the World's Columbian Exposition as a landmark achievement.[4]

Although the National Academy of Design elected two women sculptors to associate membership as early as 1828 and 1842, they were considered amateurs and did not advance to permanent status. The next election of a woman did not occur until 1906 when Bessie Potter Vonnoh became a member of the Academy. By contrast, in 1899, the six-year-old National Sculpture Society had admitted three women: Theo Ruggles Kitson, Enid Yandell and Bessie Potter Vonnoh.

The Paris *Salon* was the pinnacle of exhibition possibilities of the nineteenth century. A woman's work not only had a greater chance of being accepted for exhibition there than in the United States, but also had a chance of winning an award. In 1889 Theo Ruggles Kitson was the first American woman sculptor to win an award at the *Salon*. Fourteen other American women exhibited there before 1900, including Edith Howland and Clio Hinton Bracken.

Anna Hyatt's experience at the 1910 *Salon* was somewhat different. Her full-scale model for a life-size *Joan of Arc* was awarded first place; however, the judges withdrew the award and gave an honorable mention because they did not believe a woman could have done all the work without male assistance. But, the sculptor had completed the entire work alone—from building the armature to emplacing more than one ton of clay—a process she described as "a terribly brutal piece of work."[5]

In his 1921 book, *Modern Tendencies in Sculpture*, Lorado Taft devoted chapters to Rodin, Saint-Gaudens,

and sculpture from France, Germany, America and "various lands."[6] Although four women—Edith Burroughs, Anna Hyatt (later Huntington), Evelyn Longman and Gertrude Vanderbilt Whitney—were mentioned in the chapter on American sculpture, none received in-depth analysis. In fact, only five sentences on American women sculptors appeared in the entire volume and only one work by a woman was pictured, though there were more than four hundred illustrations. Yet, Taft was well aware of the existence of women in the sculpture profession since many of them had studied with him. He even championed their cause during the 1893 World's Columbian Exposition when he asked permission to employ women as his assistants—the famous "White Rabbits."[7] Despite vast experience with women as artists, Taft's lack of recognition of their accomplishments was not uncommon.

Janet Scudder (1873-1940), brought up in Terre Haute, Indiana, was adventurous and uninterested in what were considered proper female pursuits. While working as one of Taft's White Rabbits, she was greatly impressed by the exuberant sculpture of Frederick MacMonnies which she saw at the 1893 Fair. Setting out for Paris with the painter Zulime Taft, sister of Lorado Taft, Scudder eventually persuaded MacMonnies to accept her as an assistant. On a trip to Italy she saw for the first time the Renaissance sculpture of Donatello and Verrocchio: a pivotal influence in her work. Her first sculpture produced in this period, *Frog Baby* or *Frog Fountain*, a little boy dancing in delight, was purchased by Stanford White for use in the elaborate homes he designed for his clients. With this patronage Scudder's career was firmly established and her work was bought up as quickly as she could produce it.

Although she had several commissions for monuments, Scudder was considered the major progenitor of garden sculpture in America. In a newspaper interview she explained why she disdained public monuments:

Washington has been almost disfigured by equestrian statues...You can hardly look in any direction, but a huge bronze figure intervenes...If I had my way I would make it a law that no more of them should be placed there or in any city which makes pretensions to municipal beauty.[8]

Scudder participated in the woman's suffrage movement, as did a number of her female colleagues. Late in life after she became dissatisfied with the lack of color in sculpture, she turned her talents to painting.

Gertrude Vanderbilt Whitney (1877-1942) was mentioned in Taft's *Modern Tendencies in Sculpture*, however he referred to her by her husband's name—Mrs. Harry Payne Whitney—since she was both a sculptor and a prominent member of society. Throughout her life she fought to create her art. At first, with her family, the battle was to become an artist; then, with her fellow artists, she struggled to be taken seriously. Just as those of Anna Hyatt Huntington's, her contributions to art go far beyond her body of work. She used her wealth and connections to further the careers of other artists and, all too often, to provide subsistence for them. The Whitney Studio Club, established in her Macdougall Alley studio in 1914, gave artists a place to create and exhibit their work. Whitney amassed an extensive collection of American art through this patronage and, in 1930, the Whitney Museum of American Art was founded. It was not surprising that the first director of the museum was a woman – Juliana Rieser Force – described as "the dynamo that moved Gertrude Whitney's activities in art forward."[9] The museum was the first in the country to promote American art and played a major role in raising it to a position of world leadership.

Marriage was a formidable obstacle to a woman's career, even when the spouse was an artist. Elsie Ward Hering (1872-1923) gave every indication that she could become a great sculptor, but devoted some of her most productive years to assisting her husband with his art. Born on a farm in Missouri, she was brought to Denver, Colorado, by her family in 1887. After beginning her training with local artists, Hering went to New York to attend the Art Students League in 1896. Her teachers, Augustus Saint-Gaudens and Daniel Chester French, encouraged her to go to Paris. Two years later, she established a studio there and modeled *Boy and Frog*, which won a bronze medal at the 1904 Louisiana Purchase Exposition in Saint Louis.

In 1900 Saint-Gaudens invited her to work in his studio at Cornish, New Hampshire. For the next ten years she assisted him with many of his most important commissions. Along with Frances Grimes, another talented studio assistant, Hering finished some of Saint-Gaudens' projects underway at the time of his death. Her completion of the George Baker Memorial in Kensico Cemetery, New York, was praised for its "astonishingly beautiful and poetic result, filled with the spirit of his work."[10] However, after her 1910 marriage to Henry Hering, another assistant in Saint-Gaudens' studio, she helped her husband become a successful sculptor and produced little work of her own.

Edith Woodman Burroughs (1871-1916) entered the Art Students League at the age of fifteen to study modeling with Augustus Saint-Gaudens and drawing with Kenyon Cox. By the time she was eighteen, Burroughs supported herself by creating decorative figures for Tiffany and Company. Although her work was well respected, after her marriage in 1893 she subordinated her career to that of her husband, Bryson Burroughs, a painter whom she had met at the Art Students League. Unfortunately, her output was cut short in 1916 when she died at the age of forty-four from influenza. In 1917 Taft cited her as "gifted and lamented" when he wrote of her *Fountain of Youth,* which was awarded a silver medal,

and *Fountain of the Arabian Nights* for the 1915 Panama-Pacific Exposition.[11] Burroughs' sculpture at Brookgreen, *Bacchante,* a small figure seductively eating grapes, has the richness of detail stemming from the influence of the French sculptor, Injalbert.

The women sculptors of today have tread pathways cleared by their predecessors, but, in many ways, obstacles continue to exist. Although today's professional art organizations are now open to everyone, regardless of gender, women still have difficulty with public acceptance and promotion of their work, and with the identification and cultivation of patrons.

In the 1980s, the Guerrilla Girls, an anonymous group of women calling themselves "the conscience of the art world," began to speak out against the double standard in art by installing posters on buildings in New York City documenting discriminatory practices in galleries and museums. A poster from 1987 asked the direct question:

> When racism and sexism are no longer fashionable, what will your art collection be worth?...,

followed by the answer:

> ...The art market won't bestow mega-bucks on the work of a few white males forever. For the 17.7 million you just spent on a single Jasper Johns painting, you could have bought at least one work by all of these women and artists of color...

This statement preceded a list of 67 names including sculptors Anna Hyatt Huntington, Edmonia Lewis, Augusta Savage and Meta Warwick Fuller. The poster also listed thirteen tongue-in-cheek advantages of being a woman artist, such as "not having to be in shows with men," "working without the pressure of success," "being included in revised versions of art history" and "not having to undergo the embarrassment of being called a genius."[12]

Among the group of sculptors emerging in the post-World War II era, Leonda Finke (born 1922) has made a name for herself with powerful, serenely expressive images, primarily of women, that call forth an emotional response from the viewer. A versatile artist, Finke has experimented with nontraditional shapes and subject matter. Recent large-scale figures are comprised of built up layers of plaster over a metal armature. The sculpture is then carved, creating form and rough surfaces, then cast in bronze. When asked why she focuses on women as subjects she has stated: "It's very much mine. I know from a woman's experience and do what I know."[13]

Having built a reputation as an abstract expressionist in the 1950s, Audrey Flack (born 1931) moved into photorealism in the 1960s and became known for huge canvases filled with feminine and masculine icons symbolizing both the spiritual and literal interpretations of life. In the 1980s she stopped painting and began to create sculpture using the female imagery of the goddess, incorporating interpretations of classical mythology with twentieth century symbols such as rockets, bullets and airplanes. In her book, *Art & Soul, Notes on Creating,* Flack candidly observed the difficulties and the joys of being an artist, a woman, and a woman artist in today's society.

In the catalogue of her 1995 retrospective exhibition, Glenna Goodacre underscored that women artists are called upon to fulfill multiple roles in life while balancing the pressures of their work:

> My success as a sculptor was not without difficulties, but every situation provided a learning opportunity...When my work (or my gender) was rejected from a show, I allowed my anger to push me harder... I have been a student, homemaker, wife, daughter, mother, friend, home-builder, decorator, socialite, speaker, business woman, and cook—all while I was juggling my art career. It was most important to me to be recognized as a "professional artist!"[14]

Both Leonda Finke and Audrey Flack have remarked that Anna Hyatt Huntington's monumental sculpture, *El Cid Campeador,* and its companion pieces on Audubon Terrace at Broadway and West 155th Street, New York City, were an early inspiration and catalyst for their artistic interests. Audubon Terrace is the center of a complex of museums and institutions created by Archer Huntington whom Anna Hyatt married in 1923. Other women artists who claimed Anna Hyatt Huntington (1876–1973) as mentor and role model included Brenda Putnam, Sylvia Shaw Judson, Katharine Lane Weems and Marjorie Daingerfield. Hundreds of others, male and female, benefited from her patronage through acquisition of their works for Brookgreen Gardens and her many, often anonymous, contributions to the nation's art organizations, schools and museums.

Another monument by Huntington, *Joan of Arc,* at Riverside Drive and 93rd Street, New York City, has been a visual magnet for artists since its dedication in 1915. Although it was the first equestrian monument of a woman by a woman, *Joan* is significant for another reason. It was the first sculpture to represent Joan of Arc in the appropriate arms and armor. For this accomplishment Huntington was made a chevalier of the Legion of Honor by the government of France. Lorado Taft praised *Joan of Arc* for its "very great dignity," calling it "one of the notable achievements of recent years [confirming] a solidly built reputation."[15] Today, it is considered to be one of the finest monuments in America.

In founding Brookgreen Gardens in 1931 with her husband Archer, Anna Huntington set out to acquire the work of American figurative sculptors. Although not entirely by design, she collected a significant number of works by women. Brookgreen Gardens was named a National Historic Landmark in 1992 to recognize Anna Hyatt Huntington's contribution to American art through her sculpture and her patronage of women artists and to designate Brookgreen Gardens' status as an important site in women's history.

NOTES:
1. Rubinstein, Charlotte Streifer, *American Women Sculptors, A History of Women Working in Three Dimensions* (Boston: G. K. Hall & Co., 1990) 56.
2. *Ibid.,* 24. Henry James called them "that strange sisterhood who at one time settled upon the seven hills in a white marmorean flock." Led by the actress Charlotte Cushman, they included Edmonia Lewis, Emma Stebbins, Harriet Hosmer, Anne Whitney, Louisa Lander, Vinnie Ream, Margaret Foley, Blanche Nevin, Florence Freeman and Sarah Fisher Clampitt Ames.
3. *Ibid.,* 44-45.
4. Pisano, Ronald C., *One Hundred Years: A Centennial of the National Association of Women Artists* (Roslyn Harbor, N.Y.: Nassau County Museum of Fine Art, 1988) 10.
5. Humphries, Grace, "Anna Vaughn Hyatt's Statue," *International Studio,* Vol. 62, (December 1915): 48.
6. Taft, Lorado, *Modern Tendencies in Sculpture* (Chicago: University of Chicago Press, 1921), [v].
7. Scudder, Janet, *Modeling My Life* (New York: Harcourt, Brace & Co., 1925) 58. When Taft told Daniel Burnham, the chief architect of the fair, that he wanted to employ women among his assistants in order to complete the work on time, Burnham supposedly replied: "Hire any one who can do the work...white rabbits, if they will help out." His group of female assistants became known as the "White Rabbits." Among them were Edith Woodman Burroughs, Janet Scudder, Bessie Potter Vonnoh, Enid Yandell, Carol Brooks and Julia Bracken.
8. *Ibid.,* 155, 292-293.
9. Friedman, B. H., *Gertrude Vanderbilt Whitney* (Garden City, N.Y.: Doubleday & Company, Inc., 1978), 532.
10. Saint-Gaudens, Augustus, *The Reminiscences of Augustus Saint Gaudens,* vol. 2 (New York: 1913), 354-355.
11. Taft, *Modern Tendencies,* 140.
12. Chadwick, Whitney, *Women, Art, and Society* (New York and London: Thames and Hudson, 1990), 351.
13. Poole, Joan Lauri, "Bound and Unbound: Leonda Finke's Heroic Women," *Sculpture Review* 44, no. 3 (Winter 1996), 9.
14. Edson, Gary, ed., *Glenna Goodacre: The First 25 Years, A Retrospective Exhibition of Sculpture* (Lubbock, TX: Museum of Texas Tech University, 1995), 9.
15. Taft, *Modern Tendencies,* 131.

The Fountainhead:
The Genesis of American
Garden Sculpture

by Lauretta Dimmick
with research assistance by Marie Adams

The history of statuary created for American gardens during the "Country Place Era"— roughly the mid-1880s to the beginning of World War II—has never been adequately studied.[1] Although there continues to be an abundance of books delineating the how-tos or the history of American gardening and gardens, little scholarly attention has been given to the sculptures that adorned many of the country estates built during this period.[2] The monumental industry of designing and building of these sometimes immense houses and gardens could have spawned an equally important chapter in the history of American sculpture, but it seems, from a preliminary search that the majority of statuary gracing these man-made landscapes were imported copies of European— mostly antique or Renaissance—figures.

Although this essay cannot fully address the phenomenon that American estate gardens were predomi-nantly adorned with copies of European sculpture and the consequential negative impact this had on American sculptors, nor can it address the lacunae in the history of this genre within American sculpture, a few observations can be made. Several works in the Brookgreen Gardens collection offer the perfect foray into this largely uncharted territory.

Stanford White initiated the interest when he commissioned the young Frederick MacMonnies (1863-1937) to create a bronze statue to serve as a focal point in the vast garden complex of the estate known as "Rohallion" (Gaelic for "little red hill") which White and landscape architect Nathan F. Barrett, had designed for the New York banker Edward Dean Adams, at Seabright (now Rumson), New Jersey.[3] White, and his client Adams wanted a fountain figure for the center of a stone basin White designed, located at a driveway *rond-point* in front of the house. MacMonnies' delightful bronze *Pan,* a life-size standing figure of a young boy piping his double reeds, completed in 1890, was the inspired creation. The statue was so fashionable that MacMonnies made a tidy profit for himself by selling reductions of the figure at jewelry stores in New York City and Boston well into the 1920s. So popular was this first important American fountain figure that a photograph of it appeared on the title page of Guy Lowell's esteemed book, *American Gardens,* published in 1902. A reduction of *Pan of Rohallion* was placed in a small basin in Frank Squier's estate "Ashford" in Greenwich, Connecticut, and a photograph of this smaller fountain was illustrated in the even-more successful book, *American Estates and Gardens,* published in 1904 by Barr Ferree. Interestingly, the sculptor and sculpture were not identified in this latter book, perhaps suggesting that *Pan of Rohallion* and its maker were very well-known. At any rate, MacMonnies and White thus laid the groundwork for a new genre within the field of American sculpture.

Although Brookgreen Gardens does not own a *Pan of Rohallion* nor any of the other fountain figures MacMonnies created,[4] the collection does include a reduction of another MacMonnies figure, the infamous *Bacchante and Infant Faun,* which at one point *became* a fountain sculpture. Created during the height of his career, the *Bacchante* was neither fashioned for a commission nor as a fountain figure. Inspired by a particular model, MacMonnies sculpted this zestful figure and presented the original, over-life-size bronze to Charles McKim, one of Stanford White's colleagues in their incredibly successful architectural firm, McKim, Mead & White. McKim had lent MacMonnies money when the young sculptor first went to study in Paris many years earlier, and MacMonnies' gift of *Bacchante* was a later expression of gratitude. At the time, McKim, Mead & White, was just completing Boston's new Public Library in the neo-Renaissance style; an inner courtyard featured a basin waiting for a sculpture to be its focus. McKim offered to give MacMonnies' *Bacchante and Infant Faun*

Pan of Rohallion by Frederick William MacMonnies (1863-1937), 1890. From "American Gardens" (Guy Lowell), courtesy of Denver Art Museum, Denver, Colorado.

to the Library; the Library's Trustees accepted and the sculpture was placed in the courtyard fountain. Although it looked beautiful with jets of water splashing over it, an incredible brouhaha erupted over the fact that the statue depicted a "naked" (not nude) female who was an associate of Bacchus, the pagan god of wine. The history of the work's initial acceptance and the subsequent condemnation and disapproval is too long to tell here.[5] In the end, McKim withdrew the sculpture and in May 1897 gave it to The Metropolitan Museum of Art in New York. Despite its travails in Boston, the sculpture, with its lightness and verve, had many admirers and MacMonnies found a ready market for reductions of it, just as he had previously with small-scale bronze replicas of the *Pan of Rohallion.* The work in the Brookgreen collection is just such an example, as would have been sold by Theodore B. Starr or Tiffany and Company in New York.

Although MacMonnies did create a few more sculptures for domestic gardens, and his *Pan of Rohallion* set the tone for many subsequent figures of fauns, Pan, and other mischievous children created by other sculptors for American estate gardens, MacMonnies' career followed the traditional pattern of working towards attaining commissions for large public monuments. We must look to one of his students, then, for a sculptor who epitomized the creator of domestic garden sculpture. Janet Scudder (1869-1940) was the American garden sculptor *par excellence.*[6] Hers is a rags-to-riches story, based on her talent, hard work, good promotion and commissions. Born to a poor family in Indiana, she eventually, by virtue of her garden sculpture, lived on her own at her villa outside Paris.

Working as an assistant in MacMonnies' Parisian studio, Scudder was one of the first American sculptors to note this genre within her mentor's work, and she would go on to make it her special theme. Another critical influence on Scudder's oeuvre was her trip to Italy during the winter of 1899-1900. In Florence she saw Donatello's *Cantoria* (1433-39) at the Museo dell'Opera del Duomo, Florence, popularly called the *Singing Boys,* and, perhaps most importantly, Andrea del Verrochio's *Putto with Dolphin* (c. 1470) at the Palazzo Vecchio, Florence. This latter fountain, with its chubby canon of proportions, was to have enormous impact not only on Scudder's work, but on the entire subsequent history of American garden statuary. Upon seeing these Italian works and others, Scudder wrote:

> I knew now what I wanted to do....I filled my brain and my sketch book...with all those gay pagan figures....My work should please and amuse the world....My work was going to decorate spots, make people feel cheerful and gay — nothing more![7]

The stage was set for Scudder to epitomize the creator of fountain statuary for American estates.

After returning to her Paris studio, fresh with ideas gathered in Italy, Scudder attempted to capture what she called the "joyousness" of her Italian prototypes when she modeled her first garden figure in 1901, *Frog Fountain,* also titled *Frog Baby,* a reduction of which is in the Brookgreen collection. In Scudder's autobiography, she told the story of how this charming, life-size figure of a young boy splashing in water sprayed on him by three frogs at the base and with water lilies woven into his tousled curls, came about. In Paris, "a little boy of four," one of many young children who were constantly asking for modeling jobs, gained entrance to her studio:

> He stood there timidly, looking at me though anxious, pleading eyes....He was so cunning and appealing [that I]...called him to me....How little I knew at that moment that he was Fate in disguise —rushing straight into my arms![8]

The child was so happy to be given a sandwich and have the chance to model that he began dancing about, "chuckling delightedly to himself all the time." Scudder continues:

> In that moment a finished work flashed before me. I saw a little boy dancing, laughing, chuckling all to himself while a spray of water dashed over him. The idea of my Frog Fountain was born.[9]

When the bronze cast was finished in Paris, Scudder eagerly sought MacMonnies' opinion about her newest work. He liked it and asked her what she planned to do with it. She replied, "Take it to New York—and start out on my career of designing fountains for gardens—for courtyards—for terraces."[10]

She did take her sculpture to New York and awaited the chance to show it to Stanford White. She was very enterprising about this and never gave up although at times it seemed she could never get his attention. When by chance she literally bumped into him on a busy New York intersection, he said he had seen her statue, and "I like it. How much do you want for it?" She replied with all her courage, "a thousand dollars," and was stupefied when he said "I'll take it. Send it to my office."[11] White told her he planned to put one replica in "the Chapin house" and another on the grounds of the James L. Breese estate in Southampton, New York.[12] White, who later put a replica of the *Frog Fountain* on his own Long Island estate, also asked Scudder to design two other fountains. At the zenith of his career as the architect of public and private buildings — and especially country estates—White was the contact Scudder needed to launch her career. As she related, "When I eventually...became more or less the fashion in garden sculpture, my telephone used to ring from nine o'clock in the morning until ten at night."[13] *Frog Fountain* established her

Putto with Dolphin by Andrea del Verrochio, c. 1470. Photograph courtesy of Art Resource, Alinari, New York City.

reputation and enjoyed continued popularity throughout her career. She was especially honored in 1906 when Daniel Chester French acquired a replica of it for the collection of The Metropolitan Museum of Art. After five life-size bronze casts were produced, she made multiple editions in three reduced sizes.[14] By 1919 at least fifty of these had been cast.[15] To give the contemporary reader some sense of the prices such sculptures commanded during the "Country Place Era," a bronze cast of *Frog Fountain,* complete with an electric pump and basin, could be had for $350.00; the figure alone sold for $200.00.[16]

MacMonnies created very important and seminal works for American garden statuary, but his career followed the traditional path of moving on to procure commissions for large public monuments. Scudder had no intention of doing the same, even very early in her career. Before her success with *Frog Fountain* she had been considered as the artist for a heroic statue of Henry Wadsworth Longfellow to be placed in Washington, D.C. She said "It would be a crime to put up another portrait statue in Washington," and asked if she could execute a fountain to memorialize Longfellow, complete with benches for sitting amidst flowers and plants. Her would-be benefactor said she didn't understand—he wanted a portrait statue. Scudder's response clearly conveyed her convictions:

> Well—I won't do it!...I won't add to this obsession of male egotism that is ruining every city in the United States with rows of hideous statues of men-men-men — each one uglier than the other — standing, sitting, riding horseback — every one of them pompously convinced that he is decorating the landscape.[17]

When Scudder found in Italy her métier for fountain figures, she recognized it and was satisfied. In so doing, she elevated the status of garden statuary and paved the way for other sculptors of her generation to work within this genre. Many works in the Brookgreen Gardens collection descend from the success that MacMonnies— and especially Scudder — established for this field and several works in the current exhibition are related to this phenomenon.

NOTES:
1. The "Country Place Era" is sometimes dated from mid-1880s to the years after the stock market crash in 1929. A recent study, however, extends the era to the beginning of World War II. See Mac Griswold and Eleanor Weller, *The Golden Age of American Gardens, Proud Owners, Private Estates, 1890-1940* (New York, 1991).
2. Griswold and Weller, *The Golden Age*, has a good bibliography of books published during the "Country Place Era," as well as more recent studies of gardening and gardens. The only studies of which I am aware on the history of American sculpture created for these estates are *Fauns and Fountains: American Garden Statuary, 1890-1930,* (Southampton, N.Y.: The Parrish Art Museum, 1985) and *Long Island Estate Gardens,* (Greenvale, N.Y.: Hillwood Art Gallery, 1985).
3. For the most recent discussion of *Pan of Rohallion* see Smart, Mary, *A Flight with Fame, the Life and Art of Frederick MacMonnies (1863-1937), with a catalogue raisonné by E. Adina Gordon* (Madison, Connecticut: 1996).
4. For information on the several fountain figures MacMonnies designed see Smart, *A Flight with Fame.*
5. Much has been written about the history of this sculpture; most recent scholarship includes Smart, *A Flight with Fame,* and Fairbanks, Jonathan, "MacMonnies' Bacchante: Its Trial, Condemnation and Restoration" *Sculpture Review* 43, no. 2 (second quarter 1993). In 1993, for the occasion of the hundredth anniversary of the Boston Public Library, a bronze cast of this sculpture was made for the Library.
6. For information on Scudder and her career see Rubinstein, Charlotte Streiffer, *American Women Sculptors* (Boston: G.K. Hall & Co., 1990) 99-100, 148-53; Conner, Janis C. and Joel Rosenkranz in *Rediscoveries in American Sculpture: Studio Works, 1893-1939* (Austin, Texas: University of Texas Press, 1989) 151-160 and *Fauns and Fountains.* Scudder's autobiography, *Modeling My Life,* (New York, 1925) is the source for all the subsequent quotes.
7. Scudder, *Modeling,* 165.
8. *Ibid.,* 171.
9. *Ibid.,* 172.
10. *Ibid.*
11. *Ibid.,* 187-88.
12. *Ibid.,* 196-97.
13. *Ibid.,* 190.
14. *Fauns and Fountains,* n.p.
15. Hill, May Brawley, *The Woman Sculptor, Malvina Hoffman and Her Contemporaries* (New York: Berry-Hill Galleries, Inc., 1984) 49.
16. *Ibid.*
17. Scudder, *Modeling,* 155.

ACKNOWLEDGMENTS:
I would like to acknowledge several persons who were helpful in assisting with the research of this essay: Marie Adams, Beryl Bowen, and Frances Derstine of the Denver Art Museum; the staff of the Interlibrary Loan, Magazines and Circulation Department of the Denver Public Library; Jeni Sandberg and Katherine Voorsanger of The Metropolitan Museum of Art; Keith Morgan and Rebecca Davidson. Christine Hennessey, Coordinator of the Inventories of American Paintings and Sculpture at the National Museum of American Art was very helpful. I am also grateful to Thayer Tolles who generously shared research material on some of the sculptors mentioned herein; the material is from the forthcoming collection catalogue on which Ms. Tolles and I (along with two other authors) have been working.

AMERICAN MASTERS
Sculpture from Brookgreen Gardens

Exhibition Catalogue

Thomas Ball

Born 1819, Charlestowne, Massachusetts
Died 1911, Montclair, New Jersey

The death of his father forced Thomas Ball to leave school and to find work to support the family. After taking a maintenance job at the New England Museum in Boston, an early interest in art that had been fostered by his father was rekindled. Ball began to copy the portraits displayed in the museum and soon opened his own business as a portrait painter and miniaturist. His fine voice enabled him to supplement this income by singing in church choirs and oratories, such as Haydn's *Creation* and Mendelssohn's *Elijah*. But Ball became increasingly disheartened as his painting career languished. John King, a friend and portrait sculptor, suggested he model clay, launching a new area of interest. A cabinet bust of the singer Jenny Lind, Ball's first serious attempt at portraiture, was an immediate success.

In 1854, Ball relocated to Italy to make sculpture a career, eventually returning for an eight-year period to Boston. Like many artists of his time, Ball was best known for realistic, yet unpretentious, portraits and monuments. Perhaps the most important of these were the heroic statue of Washington on horseback for the Public Gardens in Boston and a statuette of Henry Clay. The figure of Clay not only accurately captured the individual spirit of the man, but depicted him in appropriate clothing and posture. The equestrian of George Washington was a challenge for two reasons. Ball had not yet attempted a full-length, life-size figure, let alone an heroic figure, and the work was modeled in plaster rather than in clay. Unfortunately, by the time he completed the monument, the War Between the States was raging and all foundries were devoted to the war effort. The casting was made several years later.

In addition to his public monuments and portraits, Ball created a few ideal works. One of these, *Love's Memories*, a carving of a sweetly pensive cupid with crossed legs, seated upon an Ionic capital, draws upon Victorian sentiment. This work was done about the same time as Ball's *Emancipation Group* or *Freedman's Memorial*, a sculpture praised for its literal naturalism. The monument of Abraham Lincoln and a freed slave was placed at Washington, D.C., in 1876. By that time, Daniel Chester French had entered Ball's Italian studio as a pupil and assistant.

My Three Score Years and Ten, Thomas Ball's autobiography, is one of a few written by an artist. It reveals an intimate look at his artistic struggles and his familial and professional relationships.

SOURCES:
Craven, Wayne, *Sculpture in America* (Newark: University of Delaware Press, 1984) 219-228.
Goode, James M., *The Outdoor Sculpture of Washington, D.C.* (Washington, D.C.: Smithsonian Institution Press, 1974) 86.

Love's Memories
White marble, 1875
30 x 15 x 15 in. (78.2 x 38.1 x 38.1 cm.)
Signed: T. BALL 1875
Gift of Joseph Veach Noble in honor of
Dr. & Mrs. Joseph H. Noble

George Grey Barnard

Born 1863, Bellefonte, Pennsylvania
Died 1938, New York City

The embodiment of universal ideas in art was George Grey Barnard's driving force. Inspired by the work of Michelangelo and Rodin, he imbued his sculpture with passion and intensity. Depictions of the human figure, both beautiful and powerful, were his forte. Barnard's concern with the play of light upon the surface of his objects resulted in figures having a dream-like quality of dark and shadow, luminescence and purity. *I Feel Two Natures Struggling Within Me,* two monumental male figures, exemplified this quality. The concern with light was carried to such extent that the modeling was done in a semi-darkened room, resulting in the models' poses becoming the essence of form.

A twelve-year period in Paris (1883–1895), provided Barnard with an opportunity to focus totally upon his work and perfect his almost mystical vision of art and life. In 1894, at the Paris *Salon,* his sculpture was publicly exhibited for the first time and met with critical acclaim. One of his best known and most controversial works was a monumental figure of Abraham Lincoln commissioned for Cincinnati, Ohio. Barnard's simple directness in portraying Lincoln as a man of the people was interpreted by critics as a lack of respect for the subject and criticized for its plainness. The force and emotion portrayed through his subject matter was something that few could comprehend, leading (as in the case of his *Lincoln*) to a confusion on the part of the public as to the sculptor's intent. Barnard's singular vision brought about the cosmic ideas portrayed through his art. As one reviewer wrote, "Every manifestation of life, however fleeting, is to him fraught with a hidden meaning; the spirit that has its being in and behind things,...is at once the goal and the point of departure of all his art."

While living in France Barnard collected architectural fragments and figures of Gothic sculpture. This extensive collection was brought to the United States and installed in a structure at Washington Heights, New York. Eventually, the works were acquired by The Metropolitan Museum of Art and became the nucleus for The Cloisters.

Twenty years of Barnard's career were spent on the completion of one work, *The Rainbow Arch,* his powerful statement against war. This multi-figured composition, envisioned as a national monument to peace, incorporated the interplay of light, shadow and form that had become central to his work. At the same time, the group of more than fifty figures was presented with minimal architectural framework. Although it was to be his *tour de force,* the monumental work was left unfinished at his death.

Another example of his genius is *Maidenhood,* a serene figure that projects great energy. Barnard wrote to Archer Huntington, "This morning a clip came showing the *Maidenhood* in your Carolina gardens. I am happy to know you adopted the orphan. I finished that marble in a way I finished no other flesh." This is the only example of the full sculpture. A head in marble, carved after the figure was completed, is in the collection of the Art Institute of Chicago. According to Barnard, the pose — a candid one taken by the model at rest — was as faithful an interpretation of the living model as he could create. He described the work as being "all nature in divine balance."

SOURCES:
Dickson, Harold E., "Barnard and Norway," *The Art Bulletin,* 44 (March 1962): 55-59.
Laurvik, J. Nilsen, "George Grey Barnard," *The International Studio,* 36, no. 142 (December 1908).
George Grey Barnard to Archer M. Huntington, 29 and 30 March 1938, "Sculptor's Correspondence Files," Brookgreen Gardens Archives.
McSpadden, J. Walker, *Famous Sculptors of America* (Freeport, N.Y.: Books for Libraries Press, 1924; reprint, 1968).

Maidenhood
White marble, 1896
36 x 42 x 25.5 in. (91.4 x 106.7 x 64.7 cm.)

Paul Wayland Bartlett

Born 1865, New Haven, Connecticut
Died 1925, Paris, France

Paul Bartlett always remained connected with America, although he made France his home. His father, Truman H. Bartlett, a noted sculptor and author, moved the family to Paris to take advantage of the abundant artistic opportunities. After he began to study animal sculpture, Bartlett's early work was encouraged by Emmanuel Frémiet. He entered the École des Beaux-Arts in 1880 and also studied with Auguste Rodin. His precocious artistic talent was confirmed when a bust of his grandmother, modeled when he was twelve-years-old, was accepted for exhibition in the 1880 Paris *Salon*. At the age of twenty-four, Bartlett was invited to become a member of the *Salon* jury. Two years earlier, in 1887, he had contracted with Siot-Decauville & Perzinka to reproduce and market small versions of his work, the first known agreement between an American sculptor and a French foundry.

Although he began as an animal sculptor, Bartlett's impressionistic technique and romantic spirit evolved into an increasing interest in figure studies. Works such as the *Bohemian Bear Tamer* and *The Ghost Dancer* earned him public recognition both in France and the United States. The elegant equestrian monument of *Lafayette,* a gift of the school children of America to France, was his first public commission. Through an association with French ceramist Jean Carriès, Bartlett began in 1890 to experiment with patinas. He eventually developed brilliant color effects in small bronzes that he cast himself using the lost-wax process. Exhibited at the Louisiana Purchase Exposition of 1904 and in the *Salon*, these works aroused great public interest. This experimentation in lost-wax casting led him to play a major role in the development of its use in American bronze foundries.

Study in Bronze embodies Bartlett's special handling of the nude figure, noting the influence of Rodin. Other examples of this work are in the collections of the Pennsylvania Academy of the Fine Arts and the Musée National d'Art Moderne.

SOURCES:
McSpadden, J. Walker, *Famous Sculptors of America* (Freeport, N.Y.: Books for Libraries Press, 1924; reprint, 1968).
Proske, Beatrice Gilman, *Brookgreen Gardens Sculpture* (Murrells Inlet, S.C.: Brookgreen Gardens, 1968) 30-32.
Shapiro, Michael Edward, *Bronze Casting and American Sculpture, 1850 1900* (Newark: University of Delaware Press, 1985) 121-132.

Study in Bronze
Bronze, c. 1896
9 x 4 x 6 in. (22.8 x 10.1 x 15.2 cm.)
Gift of Bessie Potter Vonnoh

John Gutzon de la Mothe Borglum

Born 1867, near Bear Lake, Idaho
Died 1941, Chicago, Illinois

Gutzon Borglum was one of the most dynamic sculptors of the early twentieth century. Initially he studied painting and depicted scenes inspired by his western upbringing. Eventually he found his artistic niche in sculpture, experimenting with small works then later with works on a colossal scale. His paintings helped finance three years of art study in Paris at the Académie Julian and the École des Beaux-Arts, as well as travel to Holland, Belgium and Spain. His first major exhibition of paintings and small sculpture was held in London, where his depictions of American western themes met with public acclaim and led to further commissions.

During his three years in Europe, he met Auguste Rodin, an encounter that influenced Borglum's artistic direction. He discontinued the anecdotal themes of his bronze work and began to carve sensual, passionate female figures in marble. These symbolic works, such as *The Martyr* and *The Atlas,* presented universal concepts of womanhood in an enlightened manner. A shift to architectural sculpture gave him the opportunity to work on a series of figures for the Cathedral of St. John the Divine in New York City. Borglum also received commissions for public monuments that helped to ensure his reputation as an artist. The equestrian statue of General Philip Sheridan at Washington, D.C., and the statue of Abraham Lincoln at Newark, New Jersey, allowed him to present emotional intensity and sense of drama.

Borglum's imagination and energy led him into a realm of sculpture not previously undertaken in America — large scale reliefs carved across mountainsides. After initiating work on a Confederate Memorial at Stone Mountain, Georgia, disagreement with the project committee led to his abrupt departure with the relief only partially carved. Perhaps his best known work was the *Shrine of Democracy*, a group of four presidents' heads carved over a twenty-year period into the rock of Mount Rushmore in the Black Hills of South Dakota. He was unable to complete the work before his death in 1941, but it was finished by his son, Lincoln Borglum.

A study for an early piece, *Head of Nero* owes a debt to Rodin with its portrayal of intense emotion: disarray, madness, terror. The wildly staring eyes and flaccid mouth entice luridly. Borglum wrote, "Each of us puts something of his life in his work. Something in my life made my Nero possible. It has passed; it has gone out of my life. It would be impossible for me to create another Nero or to shape a being at all like him. There are days when, absorbed in my angels, my saints, I hate my Nero; but if art is worth anything at all it must be real, and he was real at the time."

SOURCES:
Mechlin, Leila, "Gutzon Borglum, Painter and Sculptor," *The International Studio*, 28 (April 1906): xl.
McSpadden, J. Walker, *Famous Sculptors of America* (Freeport, NY: Books for Libraries Press, 1924; reprint, 1968).
Proske, Beatrice Gilman, *Brookgreen Gardens Sculpture* (Murrells Inlet, S.C.: Brookgreen Gardens, 1968) 59-65.

Head of Nero
Bronze, 1902
Signed: *B . . .*
2 3/8 x 1 9/16 x 2 1/16 in. (6.1 x 4 x 5.2 cm.)
Permanent loan from the Hispanic Society of America

Solon Hannibal Borglum

Born 1868, Ogden, Utah
Died 1922, Stamford, Connecticut

Encouraged by his brother Gutzon, who was then pursuing a painting career, Solon Borglum became a sculptor. His family's life on the western frontier furnished subject matter; Rodin's powerful images and impressionistic surfaces provided examples. The success of Borglum's small bronzes — Native Americans pitted against nature and man — led to significant public commissions. As a colleague remarked, his works were mostly small in size, but big in effect.

At the outbreak of World War I, although he was too old to serve in the army, Borglum volunteered to work with the YMCA and was placed with the French Third Army providing food and comfort to weary soldiers *(foyer du soldat)*. For this work, often conducted along front lines, he was awarded the *Croix de Guerre*, an honor reserved for soldiers serving in battle. For a few months following the armistice, Borglum directed the sculpture department of an art school near Paris, operated under the auspices of the American army. His School of American Sculpture in New York City opened in 1919, six months after his return from France. Its goal was to raise sculpture in America to its proper position, using American ideas and models, rather than copying classic traditions. Drawing as the basis for form and construction was emphasized. Borglum believed that knowledge of anatomy, or at least an understanding of the form beneath the surface, was absolutely necessary for sculptors. *Sound Construction*, an art textbook based on his teaching philosophy, was published posthumously in 1923. Borglum had died of complications following a ruptured appendix in 1922.

On the Border of the White Man's Land was one of several studies made during the summer of 1899, spent on the Crow Creek Reservation in South Dakota. Under the title *The Scout*, it was accepted for exhibition in the 1900 Exposition Universelle at Paris where it received a silver medal. Borglum exhibited two other works there: a life-size bronze, *Stampede of Wild Horses*, placed at the entrance to the United States Pavilion, and *Buffalo*, recipient of a bronze medal. As a profound interpretation of a western theme, *On the Border of the White Man's Land* exemplifies the impressionistic qualities of Borglum's technique, coupled with the distinctive narrative quality of his composition. The blurred details reinforce the imagery of a horse and man perched atop a windswept overlook. The model was Black Eagle, one of Custer's scouts.

SOURCES:
Davies, A. Mervyn, *Solon H. Borglum, A Man Who Stands Alone* (Chester, Conn: Pequot Press, 1974).
Proske, Beatrice Gilman, *Brookgreen Gardens Sculpture* (Murrells Inlet, S.C.: Brookgreen Gardens, 1968) 76-79.

On the Border of the White Man's Land
Bronze, 1899
19 x 23.25 x 9.25 in. (48.3 x 59 x 23.5 cm.)
Signed: *Solon Borglum* On front: *On the Border of the White Man's Land* and *Original cast made especially for J. Morgan Jones 1918*

Alexander Stirling Calder

Born 1870, Philadelphia, Pennsylvania
Died 1945, New York City

One of the first American sculptors to emphasize the decorative qualities of his art was Stirling Calder. His method progressed from the realism of the nineteenth century toward an increased stylization of forms. He combined the spontaneity of quick imagination and a strong feeling for design with a keen sense of drama.

In Philadelphia, Thomas Eakins and Thomas Anshutz gave Calder his initial instruction at the Pennsylvania Academy of the Fine Arts. Then, in 1890, he went to Paris where he enrolled at the Académie Julian and the École des Beaux-Arts, studying with Chapu and Falguière until 1892. Some of his early works display the art nouveau style, then in vogue, and a growing predilection for fountain and garden figures. The Swann Memorial, *Fountain of the Rivers,* at Philadelphia, and the sculptural decoration for the boat-shaped island at Vizcaya, the Deering Estate in Miami, both combine whimsy and elegance in a rich composition.

Stirling Calder was acting chief of the sculpture department at the Panama-Pacific Exposition of 1915 in San Francisco where he designed the ornamental center of the South Gardens, *Fountain of Energy,* celebrating the joining of the Atlantic and Pacific Oceans by the Panama Canal. His other creations for the fair were sculpture for the Nations of the East and West, including a group of sparkling *Star Maidens* along the upper balustrade of the Court of the Universe. Calder's coordination of more than 1,500 pieces of sculpture for the exposition led him to state, "They sing in many themes, always in harmony, but with no loss of character or individuality."

Although he received commissions for architectural sculpture, this field of art did not allow his imagination free reign, and some of the spontaneity of design characteristic of his work is absent. The human figure was another area of interest. From endearing depictions of children to powerful monuments, Calder infused his figures with charm, grace, drama and vitality. *Man Cub,* a life-size portrait of his four-year-old son Alexander displays this special ability.

Epitomizing the title *Tragedy and Comedy,* the two figures of Hamlet and Touchstone in Calder's memorial to William Shakespeare juxtapose humor and drama. The decorative details — curule chair, gilded bells on the jester's cap and bauble, the curved knife placed in the hand of the tortured prince — are indicative of Stirling Calder's mastery of design and composition. The heroic bronze of this work was placed in Logan Circle, Philadelphia in 1928. Four years later, it received the McClees Prize at the exhibition of the Pennsylvania Academy of the Fine Arts.

SOURCES:
Ewald, Donna and Peter Clute, *San Francisco Invites the World, The Panama-Pacific International Exposition of 1915* (San Francisco: Chronicle Books, 1991).
Proske, Beatrice Gilman, *Brookgreen Gardens Sculpture* (Murrells Inlet, S.C.: Brookgreen Gardens, 1968) 110-114.

Tragedy and Comedy
Bronze, c. 1928
36 x 14 x 18 in. (91.4 x 35.6 x 45.7 cm.)
Signed: *Calder*

Henry Clews, Jr.

Born 1876, New York City
Died 1937, Lausanne, Switzerland

Born to a life of wealth and privilege, Henry Clews turned away from American society and inward to his own world frequented by personages symbolic of the society that he shunned. His highly intellectual art, the product of an intense emotional response to life, ran counter to that of his contemporaries.

After a brief foray into the family banking business, Clews took a studio in New York and began to paint, developing his own technique without instruction. An admiration for the work of Whistler manifested itself in paintings of black and gray tones. About 1907, Clews traveled to Paris to satisfy his sense of form by taking up sculpture. Still working independently, he produced a series of small heads in marble and bronze that were exhibited in New York in 1909. Expressing mood and character rather than exact features, these impressionistic works show the unmistakable influence of Rodin whose studio Clews frequently visited.

By 1914 he had become an expatriate, spending the period of World War I in Paris and eventually purchasing La Napoule, a château on the Bay of Cannes. Acquisition of this private retreat gave Clews complete creative freedom and allowed him to channel his energy and intellect into not only renovating, but remaking, La Napoule into his imaginary world. From 1918 until the early 1930s, Clews labored on the château and its ornamentation, carving arches, portals, capitals, corbels, urns and basins. Working in a variety of stone and wood required a change in style and technique. As a result, La Napoule's architectural sculpture and ornamentation was characterized by compact composition, stylized forms and decorative details previously not found in his work. Clews's subject matter—parts of bodies of insects, animals, birds, fish and reptiles—was reconfigured into individual creatures of fantasy, such as a frog-like body with a bird's beak, fins and feathers. He took the creative process one step further by abstracting many of the natural forms into curving decorative elements.

His friendship with Auguste Rodin encouraged Clews to create highly personal interpretations of society. But his vision, distorted by the excesses and vulgarities he perceived, was often grotesque and painfully penetrating. His early impressionistic work evolved into gross sculptural caricatures attacking materialism and conceit. In the small figure *The Duchess,* the haughty dowager's finery has been stripped away to reveal little substance underneath—both literally and symbolically. She stands naked, except for pearls and a fan, upon a base emblazoned with two flamingos mimicking her prideful attitude and stance. The ravaged body, with sagging flesh and wrinkled skin, is modeled in great detail.

After completing the work at La Napoule, Clews returned to portrait sculpture, producing heads of friends and people who lived around the château. These powerful studies exhibited skillfully modeled facial features and characteristics. None of the satirical distortions found in his earlier sculpture come forth in these later works created during the last few years of his life. He died in 1937 and was buried in a tower at La Napoule. Inscribed on his tomb is his poem: "If God grant me three score and ten, I shall be ready to depart. I shall have finished with my art and the ways and wiles of men. I hope, however, to return, but not as Ouija spook before purees, spiritists, or Marxist or scientific feminist — I yearn to come at eventide as sprite and dance upon the window sill of little folk, wide-eyed and still when summer moon is shining bright. And I shall dance with might and main to let dear little children see how quaint and funny I can be. From science I shall set them free and give them mirth and mystery and myth and fairy lore again."

SOURCES:
Proske, Beatrice Gilman, *Brookgreen Gardens Sculpture* (Murrells Inlet, S.C.: Brookgreen Gardens, 1968) 84-92.
Proske, Beatrice Gilman, *Henry Clews, Jr., Sculptor* (Murrells Inlet, S.C.: Brookgreen Gardens, 1953).

The Duchess
Aluminum, c. 1914
20.5 x 4 x 4 in.
(52.1 x 10.1 x 10.1 cm.)
Signed: *HC* [monogram]

Donald Harcourt De Lue

Born 1897, Boston, Massachusetts
Died 1988, Leonardo, New Jersey

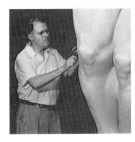

Donald De Lue was considered the dean of American sculpture when he died in 1988 at the age of ninety-one. Heroic figures comprised an important part of his work, including the American war memorial at Normandy, France, and *The Rocket Thrower* for the 1964 New York World's Fair. De Lue's work was particularly well suited to architectural settings. Portrayal of strong musculature, such as that found in archaic sculpture, strengthened the patterns of his figures. Forms took precedence over line.

De Lue studied for several years in Boston at the school of the Museum of Fine Arts, and worked with the sculptor Bela Lyon Pratt. Both Richard Recchia and Robert Baker employed him when he had gained enough skill to be useful as an assistant. Later on, he worked with Bryant Baker, brother of Robert Baker. During this period, De Lue constantly studied, acquiring a strong foundation in technique, although he had little time for his own creative work.

In the early 1940s, De Lue began to exhibit his sculpture — immediately attracting both attention and prizes. The receipt of a Guggenheim Fellowship allowed him to begin work on an ambitious project for a Hall of History although it was halted by the Korean War. During World War II he designed several works under the auspices of the Citizens' Committee for the Army and Navy, including a relief of Saint Michael in armor adopted as an emblem by commando units. A grant in 1945 from the National Institute of Arts and Letters enabled him to continue his own creative work.

The heroic monument became De Lue's signature piece. A statue of George Washington as President and Masonic Grand Master is in the New Orleans Civic Center and several other cities. A much different representation of Washington, dedicated in 1967 at Valley Forge, shows the first president kneeling in prayer. In the nation's capital, a tribute to the Boy Scouts is located between the Washington Monument and the White House. A soldier rallying his comrades as he rushes in to battle is the subject of the Confederate Memorial at Gettysburg National Military Park.

The mythical figure *Icarus* is shown as he plummets to earth, wings forced upward, mouth agape in horror. It was this ability to convey emotion and power in the design, regardless of the scale of the work, that brought De Lue a series of distinguished commissions and honors. *Icarus* won a medal of honor at the Allied Artists of America exhibition in 1946.

SOURCES:
Donald De Lue (Athens, Ga.: American Sculptors Series 15, 1955).
Howlett, D. Roger, *The Sculpture of Donald De Lue, Gods, Prophets and Heroes* (Boston: David R. Godine Publisher, 1990).
Lantz, Michael, ed., "Reminiscing with Donald De Lue," *National Sculpture Review* (Summer 1974).
Salmon, Robin R., *Brookgreen Gardens Sculpture, Volume II* (Murrells Inlet, S.C.: Brookgreen Gardens, 1993) 101-104.
Tortorella, Karen, "Donald De Lue: A Man and a Monument; Sculptor Captures Magnificent Spirit," *The New York Times* (10 December 1982).

Icarus
Bronze, 1945
30.5 x 10.25 x 7 in. (77.5 x 26 x17.7 cm.)
Signed: *De Lue 1945*

Charlotte Dunwiddie

Born 1907, Alsace-Lorraine, France
Died 1995, New York City

Charlotte Dunwiddie grew up as Elizabeth Charlotte Eugenia Natalie Klein in the household of her stepfather, Adolph Hannau, a prominent German industrialist. Their cosmopolitan lifestyle included winters in Dusseldorf and summers on an estate in Wiesbaden. By the age of seven, she already had begun to study painting, the ballet and piano. Since her stepfather owned race horses and had his own race track, she learned to ride when she was a small child and later trained her own horses. At the age of fifteen, she won her first championship in dressage.

Following her own inclinations and without formal instruction, she put to use her intimate knowledge of equine anatomy and her grasp of each horse's personality in modeling her favorite animals. When she was twenty, her work was shown to Professor Wilhelm Otto, director of the Berlin Academy of Fine Arts, and he accepted her as a pupil. Eventually seeking a change of environment, Dunwiddie moved to Madrid and studied with Mariano Benlliure y Gil.

At the outbreak of World War II, she was able to leave Spain for Buenos Aires. After additional instruction there from Alberto Lagos, she began to work indepedently, carrying out her own commissions for portrait busts and reliefs. Some of this work is in the Cardinal's Palace and the Bank of Poland in Buenos Aires. Her marriage to Stanley Dunwiddie, head of the Goodyear Tire and Rubber Company in Peru, took her to Lima where she raised horses and received commissions for portraits of diplomats, industrialists and government officials. This idyllic life ended abruptly with her husband's sudden death. She distributed all of her possessions and moved to New York in 1956. Only a year later, the Kennedy Galleries gave her a solo show which was an immediate success.

The horse was Dunwiddie's favorite subject. Her intimate knowledge, acquired through years of riding and showing, created an empathy that allowed her to give even small studies great power. Her sensitive portrayal of horse and rider led to international commissions for portraits including a series of thoroughbred champions. Among these famous horses were Bold Ruler, 1957's Horse of the Year, owned by Mrs. Harry C. Phipps, and Adios Harry, harness racing's all-time highest money winner, owned by Howard Lyons. A statue of Messenger was placed at the Aqueduct Race Track Club House in 1961. Her animal subjects were not limited to horses. A portrait of Whitneymere, Cornelius Vanderbilt Whitney's champion Aberdeen Angus Bull, was commissioned in 1957.

Although her works were correct anatomically, her goal was to capture the animal's individual personality. *Tête-á-Tête*, a pair of nuzzling horses, is a good example of her special style. This sculpture won the Artists Fund Prize for the finest sculpture in the 1972 exhibition of the National Academy of Design. By the time of her death in 1995, Charlotte Dunwiddie had received nearly every major prize in American sculpture.

SOURCES:
Salmon, Robin R., *Brookgreen Gardens Sculpture, Volume II* (Murrells Inlet, S.C.: Brookgreen Gardens, 1993) 138-142.

Tête-á-Tête
Bronze, c. 1977
16 x 15.75 x 10.75 in. (40.6 x 40 x 27.3 cm.)
Signed: *Dunwiddie*
Gift of the sculptor

Mary Abastenia St. Leger Eberle

Born 1878, Webster City, Iowa
Died 1942, New York City

Her pioneer work in depicting human beings engaged in everyday activities placed Abastenia Eberle in the forefront of the field of genre sculpture. Beginning her study in Canton, Ohio, and Puerto Rico, two posts where her army doctor father was stationed, Eberle eventually went to New York City. She enrolled at the Art Students League, where she had instruction from Kenyon Cox, C. Y. Harvey and George Grey Barnard. Money was always a problem, but after her work began to win prizes and scholarships, her tuition was paid, though food was scarce.

During this time, Eberle shared a studio with a pair of musicians and the sculptor, Anna Hyatt. The two sculptors received brief criticism from Gutzon Borglum. Eberle and Hyatt created at least two works together. *Men and Bull*, which earned a bronze medal at the 1904 Saint Louis Exposition, and *Boy and Goat* were true collaborations with Hyatt modeling the animals and Eberle the human figures. Eberle's portrait bust of Anna Hyatt, carved in stone in 1905, reveals not only a flattering likeness, but a glimpse of character. In 1907, the artists went their separate ways — Anna Hyatt to France to work for a two year period and Eberle to Italy to cast some of her sculpture.

As early as 1906, Eberle began to create figures of a social nature, predating by two years the artworks introduced to the public as part of the Ashcan School. Upon her return to New York, her sincere empathy for her fellow man and the still fresh memories of little money and food led Eberle to become a settlement worker on the Lower East Side. There she had abundant subjects for her figures. Children at play, women performing daily chores and other scenes from life on the street became her focus. Not all of these small bronzes depicted idyllic scenes. Eberle was among the first to present in sculpture the unpalatable realities of the tenements: the unemployed, elderly scavengers and child prostitutes. A growing social consciousness moved her to become actively involved in social reform and the woman's rights movement. She organized exhibitions to raise funds for suffrage and to call attention to other needs.

In 1914, concerned that her work had lost its edge, she moved from a studio in Greenwich Village to the Lower East Side. Depicting her neighbors in their daily activities — working, fighting, playing, loving — Eberle produced some of her most powerful works. Life in the tenements took its toll, however, when she became ill and was unable to work. By the 1930s, she was in financial straits and dependent upon the assistance of a former student, Virginia Hart, who cared for Eberle for the rest of her life.

The Windy Doorstep, one of her most popular works, was inspired by an image of a farm woman in Woodstock, New York, sweeping on a windy day. Embodying form and movement, it won the Barnett Prize at the 1910 exhibition of the National Academy of Design. Eberle wrote, "The piece was the expression of a subjective reality — though I myself was not aware of it at the time. Later I realized why the idea of 'sweeping something out' had been so insistent."

SOURCES:
Noun, Louise R., *Abastenia St. Leger Eberle (1878-1942)* (Des Moines, Iowa: Des Moines Art Center, 1980).
Proske, Beatrice Gilman, *Brookgreen Gardens Sculpture* (Murrells Inlet, S.C.: Brookgreen Gardens, 1968) 152-154.
Abastenia Eberle to Beatrice Gilman Proske, 7 July 1937, "Sculptor's Correspondence Files," Brookgreen Gardens Archives.

The Windy Doorstep
Bronze, 1910
14 x 6 x 4 in. (35.6 x 15.2 x 10.1 cm.)
Signed: *A. St. L - Eberle*

James Earle Fraser

Born 1876, Winona, Minnesota
Died 1953, Westport, Connecticut

James Earle Fraser spent his youth on the frontier, an experience that created a lifelong interest in western life and provided powerful subjects for his art. The quality of childhood carvings made from chalkstone encouraged his parents to send him to classes at the Chicago Art Institute and to study with Richard Bock. The pull of Paris led Fraser in 1895 to the École des Beaux-Arts, where he studied with Falguière for three years. Augustus Saint-Gaudens recognized his talent and invited him to work on the commission for the General Sherman monument, an arrangement that continued until 1902 when Fraser opened his own studio in New York.

A series of commissions for portrait busts and reliefs, especially of children, gave Fraser the opportunity to apply to his own work a mastery of low relief learned from Saint-Gaudens. Fraser evolved into a sculptor known for grasping both the character and the individuality of his subjects. This ability is exemplified in commissions for public monuments, such as the heroic *Benjamin Franklin* for the Franklin Institute at Philadelphia, the colossal *George Washington* for the 1939 New York World's Fair and the statue of General George S. Patton for the United States Military Academy at West Point. Fraser endowed each of these commissions with a striking feeling for the personality of the subject and the monument's architectural setting.

Fraser's early works exhibited the impressionistic modeling and blurred outlines of Rodin, while later pieces became increasingly precise and formal. However, these later works never completely abandoned the seed of romanticism characteristic of Fraser's concepts.

The emotional force of Fraser's work captured the public's imagination. When he died in 1953, *The End of the Trail* was perhaps the best known sculpture in America. It was inspired by the poetry of Marion Manville Pope: "The trail is lost, the path is hid and winds that blow from out the ages sweep me on to that chill borderland where Time's spent sands engulf lost peoples and lost trails." Although a smaller version had been produced, exhibition of an enlargement in plaster at the 1915 Panama-Pacific Exposition at San Francisco, where it earned a gold medal, introduced it to America. To the public, *The End of the Trail* became known as a symbol of the decline of Native American culture at the height of American industrialism.

SOURCES:
McSpadden, J. Walker, *Famous Sculptors of America* (Freeport, N.Y.: Books for Libraries Press, 1924; reprint, 1968).
Proske, Beatrice Gilman, *Brookgreen Gardens Sculpture* (Murrells Inlet, S.C.: Brookgreen Gardens, 1968) 116-120.

The End of the Trail
Bronze, 1915
40 x 23 x 8 in. (101.6 x 58.4 x 20.3 cm.)
Signed: © *1915 J. E. FRASER. SC.*

Marshall Maynard Fredericks

Born 1908, Rock Island, Illinois

One of the most prolific sculptors of this century, Marshall Fredericks has enjoyed more than five hundred commissions. His style is individual, although there are elements reminiscent of his mentor Carl Milles. A blend of simple line and elegant portrayal is found in every facet of his work, from colossal monuments to small medals. Much of his work is large scale, designed specifically for outdoor settings—civic monuments, fountains, architectural sculpture. Fredericks has been an innovator in the use of fiberglass and non-traditional metals, such as nickel and copper, and introduced to America the sculptural and architectural applications of Norwegian Emerald Pearl Granite.

The Wings of the Morning was inspired by the 139th Psalm, verses 9 and 10: "If I take the wings of the morning, and dwell in the uttermost parts of the sea; even there shall Thy hand lead me, and Thy right hand shall hold me." In the sculpture, the hand of God cradles a human figure accompanied by a pair of swans. The combination of biblical symbolism and sleek forms has been employed by the sculptor in other works. *Wings* was commissioned as the centerpiece of an outdoor columbarium at Kirk in the Hills Presbyterian Church, Bloomfield Hills, Michigan. *Wings* is a good example of how Fredericks' works can comfortably transcend this original purpose, existing in this example, as easily in the garden as in its original ecclesiastical setting.

Persephone was the goddess of spring and queen of the underworld in Greek mythology. The daughter of Demeter, goddess of harvest, and of Zeus, king of the gods, Persephone attracted many admirers. Pluto, ruler of the underworld, was so smitten with her beauty that he abducted her, resulting in Demeter's wrathful act of world crop destruction. To appease Demeter and satisfy Pluto, Zeus decreed that Persephone would spend six months (autumn and winter) of each year with Pluto in the underworld, and six months (spring and summer) in the world above with her mother. Fredericks portrayed his *Persephone* at the moment of her ascension from the world of the dead to the realm of the living, just as a plant sprouts below ground and pushes its way up through the soil. Other castings of *Persephone* are in fountain settings at the Greek Theatre in the Cranbrook Educational Community and in the garden of the Gibbes Museum of Art, Charleston, South Carolina.

Marshall Fredericks successfully weds the principles of sculpture to the technical requirements of engineering, a knowledge acquired during his youth working with his father, a construction engineer. Further, the relationship of sculpture to architecture is very relevant to his work. As he wrote in his artistic credo in 1954: "There are several things concerning sculpture that I believe are extremely important. It must be wholly consistent and in harmony with the architecture involved, as well as being a beautiful entity within itself. It must embody a significance suitable to and expressive of the purpose and setting, and finally it must have a constructive meaning for others."

SOURCES:
Abatt, Corinne, "A Quiet Artist Leaves Giant Footprints," *The (Birmingham, Mich.) Eccentric,* (12 May 1983), Birmingham-Bloomfield Edition, 1E.
Colby, Jay Hakanson, "The Dragons of Marshall Fredericks," *The Magazine of the Detroit News,* (28 February 1982).
McLean, Evelyn G, "Marshall M. Fredericks, K.D. – Sculptor," *The University of Windsor Review* (Spring 1971) 6, no. 2, 29-45.
Sawyer, Sally, "Marshall Fredericks, Sculptor," *Detroit Home Journal,* (17 November 1983).
Who's Who in America 1986-87 (New York: Marquis Publishing. 1986).

The Wings of the Morning
Bronze, 1987
48 x 60 x 48 in. (121.9 x 152.4 x 121.9 cm.)
Signed: *MARSHALL M. FREDERICKS* ©
Gift of the sculptor
Shown at Brookgreen Gardens only.

Persephone
Bronze
52.5 x 30 x 30 in. (133.3 x 76.2 x 76.2 cm.)
Signed: *MARSHALL FREDERICKS*
Shown in the traveling exhibition only.

Daniel Chester French

Born 1850, Exeter, New Hampshire
Died 1931, Stockbridge, Massachusetts

One of Saint-Gaudens' successful colleagues, Daniel Chester French upheld the classical tradition in American sculpture. Two of his best known works, *The Minute Man* at Concord, Massachusetts, and *Abraham Lincoln* for the Lincoln Memorial in Washington D.C., have become national symbols. French, a product of the culture of New England, acquired his preliminary training from William Rimmer and John Quincy Adams Ward and worked for two years in the Florence studio of Thomas Ball. Although French's early work displayed attempts at naturalism, other pieces were more sentimental. In 1888, in Paris, he gained new insight, and from this point forward his work matured. The memorial to Martin Milmore initiated his new interpretation and marked the first appearance of the majestic angel figure that he frequently used.

This image of a female figure, beautiful yet otherworldly, reappears throughout French's work. He sometimes depicted her as a compassionate being with sweeping wings and shrouded face, such as *Benediction*. Part of a composition for a World War I memorial, the original design included the body of a soldier covered in the American flag and laid at the feet of an heroic angel for a final blessing. The memorial was never completed. The wings and position of the head and arms of *Benediction* are similar to French's *Genius of Creation* sculpted for the Panama-Pacific Exposition of 1915. This figure also appears as a memorial to Elizabeth Vaux Cresson in Saint Paul's Memorial Church at Oaks, Pennsylvania.

SOURCES:
McSpadden, J. Walker, *Famous Sculptors of America* (Freeport, N.Y.: Books for Libraries Press, 1924; reprint, 1968).

Benediction
Bronze, 1922
37.5 x 36 x 20 in. (95.2 x 91.4 x 50.8 cm.)
Signed: *D. C. FRENCH SC.* ©

Glenna Goodacre

Born 1939, Lubbock, Texas

One of the greatest contemporary sculptors of the human figure, Glenna Goodacre's special affinity is for women and children. Both the misadventures and joys of childhood have been shown through her innovative composition and expert modeling. A native Texan whose parents encouraged her early artistic inclinations, Goodacre studied painting and drawing at Colorado College and at the Art Students League in New York.

Her friendship with Forrest Fenn, the owner of a foundry in Lubbock, Texas, led to the casting of Goodacre's first piece of sculpture in 1969. This creation of a small figure of her young daughter in a ballet movement was the beginning of a gradual shift from painting to sculpture. Although she continued to paint, in the 1970s Goodacre turned increasingly to modeling small works for casting in bronze. By the end of that decade, her sculpture had received the Allied Artists of America Prize, the Lindsey Morris Memorial Award, the National Sculpture Society Member Award and the Gold Medal of the National Academy of Design. In 1981 Goodacre was elected a fellow of the National Sculpture Society and, in 1994, an academician of the National Academy of Design.

Her Vietnam Women's Memorial, dedicated in 1993 on the National Mall in Washington, D.C., convincingly portrays the horror and pathos inherent in the war. Designed to be a monument for the living, the group of four figures includes two nurses engaged in separate activities, while a third nurse supports the body of a wounded soldier. Although the scene can be viewed in its entirety, the figures within the composition are portrayed as separate vignettes, able to be viewed individually.

Goodacre often presents scenes from Native American cultural life in her sculpture. *Basket Dancer,* the study of one dancer from a life-size group of three figures, depicts a Pueblo Indian ritual in honor of the role of women. Castings of the large group are located in front of the Colorado Springs Fine Arts Center and in the Albuquerque International Airport. The maquette for this work was awarded a gold medal at the annual exhibition of the National Academy of Design in 1978.

SOURCES:
Edson, Gary, ed., *Glenna Goodacre: The First 25 Years, A Retrospective Exhibition of Sculpture* (Lubbock, Tex.: Museum of Texas Tech University, 1995).

Basket Dancer
Bronze, 1987
32 x 18 x 12 in. (81.3 x 45.7 x 30.5 cm.)
Signed: *G. Goodacre © 1987 AP*
Gift of Louis and Ann Wright

Charles Grafly

Born 1862, Philadelphia, Pennsylvania
Died 1929, Philadelphia, Pennsylvania

Charles Grafly was known for his highly individual portrait busts combining strong personality with accurate physical appearance. He also made his mark as a teacher at the Pennsylvania Academy of the Fine Arts after studying there with Thomas Eakins and Thomas Anshutz. Four years in Paris gave him an opportunity to study drawing with William Bouguereau and Fleury and modeling with Henri Chapu. His work was accepted for exhibition in the *Salon* of 1890, and won honorable mention in 1891.

Returning to Philadelphia in 1892, Grafly taught modeling at the Academy and at Drexel Institute. He produced work for all of the major expositions of the time including *Fountain of Man* for Buffalo in 1901, *Truth* for Saint Louis in 1904 and *Pioneer Mother Monument* for the Panama-Pacific Exposition of 1915. Grafly's greatest achievement in monumental sculpture was the memorial to General George G. Meade unveiled at Washington in 1927.

Grafly's genius came forth in portrait busts of artists, statesmen, historic figures, writers and military leaders. Lorado Taft described him as "...our master of portraiture....In his hands the soul gives up its secrets. The masks that men wear have for him an irresistible lure. He must penetrate them—must secure and present the spirit within." Some of these award-winning portraits were of the painter Childe Hassam, which won the Watrous Gold Medal of the National Academy of Design, of Frank Duveneck, winner of the Potter Palmer Gold Medal of the Art Institute of Chicago, and of the painter and teacher Thomas Anshutz, which received the Widener Medal of the Pennsylvania Academy of the Fine Arts.

Vulture of War, modeled in Paris during the winter of 1895, was part of a large unfinished work on the subject of war. Grafly's goal was to pit man against man in a group symbolic of death and destruction. The nude male figure representing the vulture is crouching, ready to seize his victim from behind. Referring to this work, Taft was of the opinion that "[Grafly] has shown more than once that he can model the nude far better than can most of his colleagues." The menacing brutality of the vulture comes across strongly in the composition despite the lack of a weapon or other means of death. The emotional quality of this work owes a debt to Rodin's influence. Only two castings of this work were made: this one and another owned by the sculptor's daughter.

SOURCES:
Proske, Beatrice Gilman, *Brookgreen Gardens Sculpture* (Murrells Inlet, S.C.: Brookgreen Gardens, 1968) 46-48.
Taft, Lorado, *Modern Tendencies in Sculpture* (Chicago: University of Chicago Press, 1921) 134-135.

Vulture of War
Bronze, c. 1895
32.25 x 15 x 15 in. (81.8 x 38.1 x 38.1 cm.)

Horatio Greenough

Born 1805, Boston, Massachusetts
Died 1852, Somerville, Massachusetts

Horatio Greenough was the first native-born American to devote his professional life to creating sculpture. As such, he is often referred to as the first American sculptor, although there were others who preceded him. The romantic painter, Washington Allston, whose birthplace was Brookgreen Plantation in South Carolina, provided inspiration for the budding artist. Allston also gave him an introduction to artistic theory while Greenough studied the classics and anatomy at Harvard. Training in stone carving was given by Alpheus Cary and instruction in modeling came from J. B. Binon and Solomon Willard. Allston convinced Greenough that his artistic development could only continue in Italy, and he went to Rome in 1825.

Immersing himself in the artistic life of the city, Greenough was introduced to the Danish sculptor Bertel Thorwaldsen, who provided criticism and encouragement. Greenough stayed in Rome for two years, following a grueling regimen of study and work, until illness forced a return to America. He modeled a series of portrait busts of prominent men including President John Quincy Adams and Chief Justice John Marshall. By 1828, he travelled once more to Italy with plaster models to be carved in marble and made arrangements to have this work undertaken at Carrara. Later in the year he went to the studio of Bartolini in Florence where the beauty of nature became a basis for his work. A concern for functionalism occurred throughout his career and influenced his writings on architecture.

The small head entitled *Bacchus* was Greenough's first attempt at stone carving. Created at the age of fourteen, *Bacchus* was presumed lost after Greenough gave it to Paul Trapier, a Harvard classmate from Charleston, South Carolina, in whose family it remained for more than 170 years. Although unfinished and reflecting the technique of an amateur, the work has charm and merit.

Greenough's use of compact design is a result of the small size of the original marble block. The inspiration for *Bacchus* is unconfirmed; however, it probably came from an engraving Greenough viewed at the Boston Athenaeum.

SOURCES:
Crane, Sylvia E., *White Silence: Greenough, Powers and Crawford, American Sculptors in Nineteenth-Century Italy* (Coral Gables, Fla.: University of Miami Press, 1972).
Craven, Wayne, *Sculpture in America* (Newark, Del.: University of Delaware Press, 1984).
Kasson, Joy S., *Marble Queens and Captives, Women in Nineteenth Century American Sculpture* (New Haven: Yale University Press, 1990).
Proske, Beatrice Gilman, "Horatio Greenough's Bacchus," *The American Art Journal* (May 1974): 35-38.
Thorp, Margaret Farrand, *The Literary Sculptors* (Durham, N.C.: Duke University Press, 1965).
Wright, Nathalia, *Horatio Greenough, The First American Sculptor* (Philadelphia: University of Pennsylvania Press, 1963).
_____, "Horatio Greenough's Roman Sketchbook," *The Art Quarterly*, 26, no. 3 (Autumn 1963) 323-332.
_____, ed., *Letters of Horatio Greenough, American Sculptor* (Madison: The University of Wisconsin Press, 1972).

Bacchus
White marble, c. 1819
12.25 x 5 x 4.75 in. (31.1 x 12.7 x 9.5 cm.)
Signed: *HG*
Gift of Beatrice Gilman Proske

Walker Kirtland Hancock

Born 1901, Saint Louis, Missouri

Although his work encompasses everything from monuments to medals, Hancock has a special interest in garden sculpture. The models for his figure sculpture were often Finnish immigrants, who settled near his home on Cape Ann, Massachusetts. The athletic quality of the young male body is presented with simplicity and straightforwardness. In the same manner, natural renderings of children's forms are found in many of his works for the garden.

After study with Victor Holm at the Saint Louis School of Fine Arts, Hancock attended the Pennsylvania Academy of the Fine Arts, where Charles Grafly was his teacher. There he won the Cresson Traveling Scholarship in 1922 and 1923, and was the recipient of the *Prix de Rome* in 1925. His three year period at the American Academy allowed him to study works of the Italian Renaissance and to create several elegant figures for garden settings such as *The Bag-Pipe Player* and *Boy and Squirrel.* In both 1956 and in 1962, Hancock returned to Rome as sculptor-in-residence at the Academy.

Hancock's mastery of design is evident in expressive compositions for memorial commissions received after World War II. His three angels of victory were placed atop the tower at the Lorraine American Cemetery at Saint-Avold, France. An heroic angel of the resurrection, raising the limp body of a soldier out of the flames of war, served as a memorial to the employees of the Pennsylvania Railroad, at the 30th Street Station in Philadelphia.

In 1966, some fifty years after its inception by Gutzon Borglum, Walker Hancock completed the carving of the Confederate Memorial across the face of Stone Mountain, Georgia. He was the third sculptor to have directed work at that site. Although it is the largest bas-relief sculpture in the world, it was considerably modified from Borglum's original concept. Hancock proposed softening down the mountain relief so that it appeared as a great granite sketch, rather than the grouping of several individual figures that Borglum had envisioned. Using thermo-jet torches to carve away the granite, Hancock was able to remove tons of stone quickly, in contrast to the older methods.

Boy and Squirrel was modeled while Hancock was a student at the American Academy in Rome. The idyllic scene, a smiling boy tempting a cautious squirrel with food, is charmingly appropriate in an outdoor setting.

SOURCES:
"Hancock Exhibit Shows Range of Mediums and Subjects," Gloucester, MA: Cape Ann Historical Association 9, no. 2 (April-June 1989).
Hancock, Walker, "Sculptor for Hire," *National Sculpture Review* (Summer 1980) 7-9, 25.
Proske, Beatrice Gilman, *Brookgreen Gardens Sculpture* (Murrells Inlet, S.C.: Brookgreen Gardens, 1968) 352-354.
"The Great Stone Faces," *Time* (5 August 1966) 66.

Boy and Squirrel
Batesville marble, 1928
38 x 38 x 19 in.
(96.5 x 96.5 x 48.2 cm.)
Signed: *WALKER HANCOCK*

Malvina Cornell Hoffman

Born 1885, New York City
Died 1966, New York City

Although Malvina Hoffman followed the example of her teacher, Rodin, giving vitality and emotion to her creations, she was strong enough to develop her own style independent of his influence. She grew up in an artistic household, the daughter of a concert pianist, and attended the Brearley School and the Art Students League. Studies with George Grey Barnard and Herbert Adams laid a foundation that was strengthened by criticisms from Gutzon Borglum and A. Phimister Proctor, both friends of the Hoffman family.

In 1910, after the death of her father, a small inheritance allowed Hoffman and her mother to go to Paris, where she hoped to study with Rodin. She was turned away several times before Rodin agreed to look at photographs of her work. Seeing her seriousness and the quality of her sculpture, he took her as a student. Hoffman studied with Rodin for a little over a year, then assisted in his studio until the outbreak of World War I. She also worked in the studio of Janet Scudder and was caught up in the Parisian art world. Inspired by the ballerina Anna Pavlova, Hoffman created a series of small figures of her dance moves, sometimes alone, sometimes with a partner. Eventually being allowed to make studies of Pavlova from backstage, a long-standing friendship developed between the dancer and the sculptor which bore fruit in several works. Prominent among these is a stunning twenty-six panel frieze of the *Autumn Bacchanale* modeled over a period of years.

In 1930, the Field Museum of Natural History in Chicago commissioned Hoffman to travel the world and model the racial types she encountered. After five years, the results of her trip were shown in "Races of Man," a landmark exhibition of one hundred figures. Hoffman tried to capture the moment at which each subject represented the individual characteristic of his race. *Andaman Islander* is the original model of one of those figures: "It was in the port of Rangoon that I had the good fortune to study a few little Negritos from the Andaman Islands. They were on a sailing ship, and our local adviser assured me that they were good representations of their tribes. The figure I modeled of an Andaman Islander shows the little Negrito hunter seated on a rock, trying out the elasticity of his bow. This typical weapon is of a very special design, not found in any other part of the world." *Andaman Islander* was modeled at Calcutta, one-third life-size, and enlarged at Paris for the Field Museum.

SOURCES:
Conner, Janis, *A Dancer in Relief, Works by Malvina Hoffman* (New York: The Hudson River Museum, 1984).
_____, *Malvina Hoffman (1885-1966)* (New York: Far Gallery, 1980).
Hill, May Brawley, *The Woman Sculptor: Malvina Hoffman and Her Contemporaries* (New York: Berry-Hill Galleries, Inc., 1984).
Hoffman, Malvina, *Heads and Tales* (New York: Charles Scribner's Sons, 1936) 294.
Rubinstein, Charlotte Streifer, *American Women Sculptors, A History of Women Working in Three Dimensions* (Boston: G. K. Hall & Co., 1990) 176-183.

Andaman Islander
Bronze, c. 1932
33.75 x 12.5 x 8 in. (85.7 x 31.7 x 20.3 cm.)

Anna Hyatt Huntington

Born 1876, Cambridge, Massachusetts
Died 1973, Bethel, Connecticut

Anna Hyatt Huntington's thorough knowledge of the horse, born of life-long study and keen observation, placed her in the forefront of animal sculptors. Although she was primarily self-taught, she did have some instruction from the Boston sculptor Henry Hudson Kitson, criticism from Gutzon Borglum and a brief period of study at the Art Students League.

In the first years of the twentieth century, she shared a New York apartment and studio with the *genre* sculptor, Abastenia Eberle. The two artists earned their living with small bronzes cast and marketed by Gorham Bronze. For the Saint Louis Exposition of 1904, they collaborated on two works, *Men and Bull* and *Boy and Goat,* with Hyatt modeling the animals and Eberle providing the human figures. They received a bronze medal for their efforts on the former.

By 1907 Anna Hyatt had traveled to France and taken a studio formerly occupied by the sculptor Dalou. Her first version of *Joan of Arc,* shown in plaster at the 1910 Paris *Salon,* received honorable mention. In 1914, she was commissioned to create her first monument — an equestrian of Joan of Arc for New York City. Placed in 1915, it overlooks Riverside Drive at 93rd Street.

Hyatt's vision of the charismatic saint was the first equestrian statue of a woman subject by a woman sculptor, and the first to depict her with accurate arms and armor. She described her concept: "She must have been a beautiful woman, otherwise the Dauphin of France would not have taken such a fancy to her. She must have been spiritual. She could not have been the ordinary rough peasant type. A certain fanaticism possessed her to carry her through those forced marches, riding on horseback — a thing she had never done before. I thought of her there before her first battle, speaking to her saints, holding up the ancient sword...it was only her mental attitude, her religious fervor, that enabled her to endure so much physically...That is how I thought of her and tried to model her."

Her painstaking process required making studies in clay from a nude model then adding the armor, saddle and harness. Hyatt made a total of seven trial models from small to life-size. Her commitment to historical accuracy further enhanced the realism of the work. Working in conjunction with a medieval art specialist, she studied details of arms and armor from tomb rubbings, paintings and funerary sculpture. For her achievement, Hyatt was made a Chevalier of the Legion of Honor and named an honorary citizen of Blois, France, where a second casting of the monument was placed.

SOURCES:

Anna Hyatt Huntington Papers, George Arents Research Library, Syracuse University, Syracuse, N.Y.

Eden, Myrna G., *Energy and Individuality in the Art of Anna Hyatt Huntington, Sculptor, and Amy Beach, Composer* (Metuchen, N.J.: The Scarecrow Press, Inc., 1987).

McSpadden, J. Walker, *Famous Sculptors of America* (Freeport, N.Y.: Books for Libraries Press, 1924; reprint, 1968).

Proske, Beatrice Gilman, "A Sculptor in Manhattan," *Sites* (New York: Lumen, Inc., 1987).

Weems, Katharine L., "Anna Hyatt Huntington," *National Sculpture Review* (Winter 1974).

Joan of Arc
Bronze, c. 1910
48.75 x 28.5 x 13 in. (123.8 x 72.4 x 33 cm.)
Signed: *Anna V. Hyatt*

Carl Paul Jennewein

Born 1890, Stuttgart, Germany
Died 1978, Larchmont, New York

With graceful line and composition, Carl Paul Jennewein exquisitely modeled characters from mythology and enchanting figures of children. After winning the *Prix de Rome* in 1918, his study at the American Academy reinforced his leaning toward pure outline and classical proportion. The small pieces produced at that time, including *Cupid and Crane* and *Cupid and Gazelle,* are considered among his finest works.

Upon his return to New York in 1921, Jennewein established his own studio and began to receive commissions for large-scale monuments and architectural sculpture. Statues of *Governor Endecott* for Boston and *The Puritan* for Plymouth, Massachusetts, are rendered with accurate, yet simple details. His mastery of relief resulted in commissions for decorative panels for the State Education Building, Harrisburg, Pennsylvania, and a frieze of cherubs for the Lincoln Insurance Building, Fort Wayne, Indiana. For this last work he received the architectural medal of honor at the Architecture and Allied Arts Exposition in 1927. Through his commission for mythological figures on the west pediment of the Philadelphia Museum of Art, completed in 1932, Jennewein was responsible for reviving an interest in polychromy in sculpture. With the architect Charles Louis Borie, he traveled through Greece to study the ancient technique and its use in architecture. Then, with the assistance of the ceramist Leon Solon, Jennewein developed a method that could replicate vivid colors on terracotta figures.

Jennewein's female nudes, in particular, bear the unmistakable mark of his talent. *The Greek Dance,* one of his most popular small bronzes, was modeled at Rome in 1926, during the time Jennewein was experimenting with polychromy. Portions of the drapery and head scarf of this figure were originally tinted reddish-orange on the surface of the silvered bronze in imitation of polychrome. Faint traces of color remain in the folds of the drapery.

SOURCES:
Howarth, Shirley Reiff, *C. Paul Jennewein, Sculptor* (Tampa, Fla.: The Tampa Museum, 1980).
Proske, Beatrice Gilman, *Brookgreen Gardens Sculpture* (Murrells Inlet, S.C.: Brookgreen Gardens, 1968) 305-311.

The Greek Dance
Silvered bronze, 1926
18-3/8 x 14.25 x 4-5/8 in.
  (46.7 x 36.2 x 11.7 cm.)
Signed: *C. P. JENNEWEIN*

Albert Laessle

Born 1877, Philadelphia, Pennsylvania
Died 1954, Miami, Florida

Albert Laessle chose animal sculpture as his special interest during his student days at the Pennsylvania Academy of the Fine Arts. His selection of subjects within that field, however, was not the usual, as he preferred to depict crustaceans, reptiles, insects and amphibians over the more lovely creatures of the animal kingdom.

One of his first sculptures was so realistic that he was accused of casting it from life. He wrote, "I had become so much interested in the type of subject from which I had chanced....that I took care not to depart from it entirely. I had no difficulty in obtaining turtles in Paris. At that time many families had turtles which were imported from Algiers and kept in the cellars to eat insects. Our concierge lent me his turtle, and I made a careful study which I sent to the *Salon* under the name 'Turning Turtle'.... Because of the peculiarity of the subject and the accuracy of the craftsmanship, the jury refused to believe that it was modeled."

A Cresson Traveling Scholarship allowed Laessle to spend three years in Europe, mostly working in Paris. Returning to Philadelphia in 1907, he assisted Charles Grafly for several years, eventually becoming an instructor at the Pennsylvania Academy in 1921. Laessle's meticulously detailed technique readily adapted to small bronzes and medals. A fascination with birdlife is reflected in a number of works from waterfowl to turkeys. His work received gold medals at the Panama-Pacific Exposition in 1915 and at the Philadelphia Sesqui-Centennial

Exposition of 1926.

Laessle's mastery was explained in the catalogue of the Panama-Pacific Exposition: "...No one in America has so closely studied the characteristics of frogs, turtles, lizards, crabs, beetles, katydids, fishes and barn fowls as Laessle, and he has presented his studies with something of the flavor of a humorous naturalist who observes the tragedies and comedies enacted in his little kingdom."

Depicting action while highlighting the oddity of an animal allowed Laessle to achieve a masterly decorative effect. *Penguins* received the Widener Gold Medal of the Pennsylvania Academy of the Fine Arts in 1918 and honorable mention at the Art Institute of Chicago in 1920.

SOURCES:
Panama-Pacific International Exposition, Vol 1 (San Francisco: Department of Fine Arts, 1915) 60.
Proske, Beatrice Gilman, *Brookgreen Gardens Sculpture* (Murrells Inlet, S.C.: Brookgreen Gardens, 1968) 180-183.

Penguins
Bronze, 1917
36 x 27.75 x 20.5 in.
 (91.4 x 70.5 x 52.1 cm.)
Signed: *ALBERT - LAESSLE*
 GERMANTOWN PHILA - 1917

Gertrude Katherine Lathrop

Born 1896, Albany, New York
Died 1986, Falls Village, Connecticut

Having both a mother and sister who were professional artists provided Gertrude Lathrop with a creative environment. Her mother was a landscape and still life painter and her sister, an illustrator of children's books. The three shared a studio in the family home in Albany and undoubtedly influenced one another's art. From the beginning Lathrop was intrigued by animal studies, especially of young animals. This special area of interest later evolved into commissions for portraits and medallic art.

Lathrop studied at the Art Students League with Solon Borglum, then entered his School of American Sculpture in 1920, soon after it opened. A summer of instruction in 1925 with Charles Grafly honed her instinct for line and composition. Almost as soon as she entered her work in exhibitions, it began to win awards. The imaginative flair of her sculpture is carried out with a keen sense of design and an attention to pattern and detail.

The unusual attributes of species such as hair patterns provided her with subject matter. The finely feathered tail and ears in *Saluki*, the Persian gazelle hound Sag Mal Haroun-al-Raschid of Kayenne, are prime examples of the way Lathrop incorporated these designs into her work. She wrote, "I think that I chose to model animals because of their infinite variety of form and texture and their great beauty, for even the homeliest of them have beauty."

SOURCES:
Proske, Beatrice Gilman, *Brookgreen Gardens Sculpture* (Murrells Inlet, S.C.: Brookgreen Gardens, 1968) 408-413.
Rubinstein, Charlotte Streifer, *American Women Sculptors: A History of Women Working in Three Dimensions* (Boston: G. K. Hall & Co., 1990) 170-171.

Saluki
Bronze, c. 1928
20.5 x 18 x 8.5 in.
 (52.1 x 45.7 x 21.6 cm.)
Signed: *G. K. LATHROP.* © 1928

Evelyn Beatrice Longman

Born 1874, Winchester, Ohio
Died 1954, Osterville, Massachusetts

Beginning her art studies at Chicago, Evelyn Longman was inspired by the sculptural richness of the World's Columbian Exposition and eventually enrolled in Lorado Taft's sculpture class at the Art Institute. After graduating with highest honors, Longman taught the summer class in sculpture.

In 1900, she left Chicago for New York and assisted Hermon MacNeil and Isidore Konti with their work for the Pan-American Exposition. At that time she applied to work in Daniel Chester French's studio, bringing with her a letter of introduction from his brother, William French, director of the Art Institute of Chicago. Longman, who has the distinction of being the only woman admitted as an assistant to French's studio, worked with him for three years before venturing out on her own, while their relationship blossomed into a friendship that continued until the end of French's life. Longman created ornamental eagles and wreaths on the Lincoln Memorial as her gift to the nation. A portrait relief of French, completed in 1926, shows the great sculptor seated before a frieze of his most important works.

The figure of *Victory* launched Longman's independent career by winning a silver medal at the Louisiana Purchase Exposition of 1904 in Saint Louis. The original figure was designed for the dome of Festival Hall and a reduction of this work was made later from the study. The Atlantic Fleet adopted the small version of *Victory* as a trophy.

Longman's use of rich ornamentation in architectural works and a style similar to that of Saint-Gaudens in bas-relief garnered many awards and commissions. Echoing the earlier success of *Victory,* a gilded figure, *The Genius of Electricity,* for the American Telephone and Telegraph Building in 1916, was one of her best

known creations. Now called *The Spirit of Communication,* the heroic male figure, wrapped in coils of cable, was one of the largest figures on the New York City skyline for many years. It is now exhibited in the headquarters of AT&T.

SOURCES:
Proske, Beatrice Gilman, *Brookgreen Gardens Sculpture* (Murrells Inlet, S.C.: Brookgreen Gardens, 1968) 133-137.
Rubinstein, Charlotte Streifer, *American Women Sculptors, A History of Women Working in Three Dimensions* (Boston: G. K. Hall & Co., 1990) 172-176.

Victory
Bronze, 1904
29.5 x 4 x 4 in. (75 x 10.1 x 10.1 cm.)
Signed: *EVELYN B. LONGMAN 1908*

Frederick William MacMonnies

Born 1863, Brooklyn, New York
Died 1937, New York City

Known for a sensual exuberance in his work, Frederick MacMonnies was at the heart of the Beaux-Arts movement in America. At the age of twenty-three he was employed as an assistant by Augustus Saint-Gaudens and studied in the evenings at the National Academy of Design and the Art Students League. In 1884, he went to Paris for two years, where he came under the influences of Falguière and Mercié. He once again worked for Saint-Gaudens in 1887 before establishing his own studio in France where he lived for more than thirty years. This lengthy residency closely allied his sculptural style with that of his French contemporaries while MacMonnies' talent as a painter provided him with another artistic outlet. Portraits of patrons and fellow artists along with scenes of the French countryside were produced in the Giverny studio he shared with his painter wife, Mary Fairchild, until their divorce in 1909. Yet, despite his absorption of Gallic culture, MacMonnies' sculpture was produced primarily for American patrons and collectors.

The palpable surfaces of his intricate designs translated easily into bronze fountains for gardens. Stanford White introduced MacMonnies' work to the wealthy patrons of the Gilded Age. *Pan of Rohallion,* commissioned in 1890 as part of White's design for the summer estate of Edward Adams, was the first of several fountain figures that popularized garden sculpture in America.

The *Columbian Fountain* for the 1893 World's Columbian Exposition at Chicago firmly established MacMonnies' reputation as an artist. His fanciful imagination soared in an extravaganza of allegorical female figures rowing a barge of state in tribute to Christopher Columbus. Its prominent placement as a focal point of the fair and positive public reaction helped to ensure its success.

Several of MacMonnies' joyful creations became the center of public controversy over what was considered flippant treatment of serious subject matter and unashamed sensuality of the human figure. A fine example of his work, the life-sized *Bacchante and Infant Faun* (also titled *Bacchante with Infant Faun*) both shocked and offended American viewers with its nudity and what was perceived to be a direct reference to inebriation. In 1896, when it was to be placed in the court of the Boston Public Library, the Woman's Christian Temperance Union, citing it as offensive to motherhood and decency, mounted a vigorous campaign against the sculpture. The donor ultimately withdrew the gift and gave it to The Metropolitan Museum of Art. Despite the American reaction to this work, *Bacchante* was overwhelmingly appreciated in France, where it became the first American sculpture acquired by the French Government. In 1897, it was placed in the Musée du Luxembourg in Paris. MacMonnies often cast reductions of his bronzes to make the works available to a wider audience. *Bacchante* was no exception.

SOURCES:
Gordon, E. Adina, *Frederick William MacMonnies (1863-1937), Mary Fairchild MacMonnies (1858-1946), Deux Artistes Américains à Giverny* (Vernon, France: Musée Municipal A.-G. Poulain-Vernon) 1988.
McSpadden, J. Walker, *Famous Sculptors of America* (Freeport, N.Y.: Books for Libraries Press, 1924; reprint, 1968).
Proske, Beatrice Gilman, *Brookgreen Gardens Sculpture* (Murrells Inlet, S.C.: Brookgreen Gardens, 1968) 33-36.

Bacchante and Infant Faun
Bronze, 1894
32 x 10 x 10 in. (81.3 x 25.4 x 25.4 cm.)
Signed: *F. MacMonnies 1894*
Gift of Joseph Veach Noble in honor of Lois C. Noble

Hermon Atkins MacNeil

Born 1866, Chelsea, Massachusetts
Died 1947, New York City

A flair for expressive action and picturesque use of detail mark the creations of Hermon A. MacNeil. Study with Falguière at the École des Beaux-Arts and with Chapu at the Académie Julien, gave his works a distinctive impressionistic flavor. Returning to the United States, MacNeil assisted the sculptor Philip Martiny, with decorative works commissioned by McKim, Mead & White for the 1893 World's Columbian Exposition at Chicago. Following this success MacNeil's career was launched, as he received numerous commissions for public monuments and architectural works including the *McKinley Memorial* at Columbus, Ohio, and the east pediment of the Supreme Court Building in Washington, D.C. In 1917, the Architectural League of New York awarded him its medal of honor, a medal he had designed, for the frieze of the Missouri State Capitol. His last major commission was the *Monument to the Confederate Defenders of Fort Sumter* at Charleston, South Carolina.

Hermon MacNeil was one of the first sculptors to deal with subjects from the American West. A study of a Sioux performer from Buffalo Bill's Wild West Show at Chicago sparked an interest in this theme source. After a study trip to the Southwest, Native American life and folklore was presented in a series of dramatic works produced in a studio at Rome with the funding of a Rinehart Scholarship from 1896 to 1899. Products of this period were *A Moqui Prayer for Rain, A Primitive Chant, Out from Chaos Came the Dawn* and *The Sun Vow.*

The Sun Vow depicts a young man becoming a warrior in a Sioux rite of passage. The romantic theme, variety of texture and pictorial elements made this work immediately popular. It was developed in Rome from a sketch done at Chicago. The group was awarded a silver medal at the 1900 Paris Exposition Universelle and a gold medal at the 1901 Pan-American Exposition at Buffalo. Life-size versions of this work are found in important collections across the United States, including the Art Institute of Chicago, The Metropolitan Museum of Art and the Corcoran Gallery of Art in Washington, D.C. The example owned by Brookgreen Gardens is a reduction of the larger group.

SOURCES:
McSpadden, J. Walker, *Famous Sculptors of America* (Freeport, N.Y.: Books for Libraries Press, 1924; reprint 1968) 307–326.
Proske, Beatrice Gilman, *Brookgreen Gardens Sculpture* (Murrells Inlet, S.C.: Brookgreen Gardens, 1968) 72-76.

The Sun Vow
Bronze, c. 1899
36 x 30 x 24 in. (91.5 x 76.2 x 61 cm.)
Signed: *H A MacNeill* [sic] On Base: *THE SVN VOW*

Paul Howard Manship

Born 1885, St. Paul, Minnesota
Died 1966, New York City

With consummate sense of style, Paul Manship blazed a singular path in the history of American twentieth century sculpture. While his muse was found in ancient art, his technique was based on contoured shape and floating form. Using astrological and mythological symbolism, Manship created sculpture like no other, providing trendsetting examples for admirers to emulate.

After studying with Charles Grafly and working in the studios of Solon Borglum and Isidore Konti, Manship entered the American Academy at Rome in 1907. There he developed the penchant for archaism that became characteristic of his sculpture. Upon his return to New York in 1910, he gained recognition with a series of commissions for private estates. These early works were marked by an exuberant lightness of form. Subsequent pieces with less detail and simplified line acquired more solidity. This later style translated well into animal sculpture, including the decorative figures for the Paul Rainey Memorial Gate at the New York Zoological Society.

For the 1939 New York World's Fair, Manship's centerpiece was a huge sundial, *Time and the Fates of Man*, and the accompanying *Moods of Time* — four dreamy figures representing *Morning, Day, Evening* and *Night*. Manship's poetic imagination comes to the fore in the floating figure of *Evening*. In *The Flight of Europa* the female figure, Europa, is presented on the back of a bull, while Eros flies alongside, whispering in her ear. Described by Stanley Casson: "It is inspired by several Minoan works of art, chief among them the bulls on the famous gold cups from Vaphio. But the inspiration has not tyrannized over the artist for, from these Minoan sources, he has made an original work of great rhythm. The triangular shape of the whole composition brings with it great subtleties of balance in weight and in line."

SOURCES:
Casson, Stanley, *XXth-Century Sculptors* (London: 1930) 53.
Proske, Beatrice Gilman, *Brookgreen Gardens Sculpture* (Murrells Inlet, S.C.: Brookgreen Gardens, 1968) 285-294.

Evening
Bronze, c. 1939
44 x 67 x 12 in. (111.8 x 169.2 x 30.5 cm.)
Signed: *EVENING Paul Manship sculp. 1938*
Shown at Brookgreen Gardens only.

The Flight of Europa
Gilt bronze, 1925
22 x 11.75 x 8.25 in. (55.9 x 29.8 x 21 cm.)
Shown in the traveling exhibition only.

Isidore Margulies

Born 1921, Vienna, Austria

Super realism is the field of Isidore Margulies. He became a sculptor in the 1970s after thirty years in another profession. Even though his first kinetic and abstract pieces were well received, Margulies has become known for his sculpture of the female nude. These figures are praised for their sensuality and elegance. Using contrasting surface textures and patinas, he creates a figure of startling realism.

Debbie II seems to defy gravity as she leans against a rail suspended in midair. This sculpture received the Gold Medal at the 1980 exhibition of the National Sculpture Society. Only the second figure of this size to be created by Margulies, it followed *Debbie*, a seated nude pulling a sweater over her head. Margulies uses form, gesture, color — through the addition of patina — and the space around the work to create his total effect. He states, "what isn't in the sculpture is as vital as what is. I want the viewer's eye to fill in those details that I have left out."

SOURCES:
Salmon, Robin R., *Brookgreen Gardens Sculpture, Volume II* (Murrells Inlet, S.C.: Brookgreen Gardens, 1993) 155-158.

Debbie II
Bronze, 1979
54.5 x 25.75 x 25 in. (138.4 x 65.4 x 63.5 cm.)
Signed: *DEBBIE II © 8/15 12/79 I.MARGULIES*

Edward Francis McCartan

Born 1879, Albany, New York
Died 1947, New York City

A close kinship with the art of eighteenth century France, especially the work of Houdon, set McCartan apart from his fellow sculptors. Study in France at the École des Beaux-Arts with Injalbert was supplemented by training at the Art Students League under George Grey Barnard and Hermon MacNeil, and at the Pratt Institute with Herbert Adams. Brilliant line and fastidious attention to detail marked McCartan's work after 1920.

McCartan's interest in perfecting ornamental design resulted in his affiliation with the school of the Society of Beaux-Arts Architects, a training ground for carving and decorative modeling. The life-size gilded figure *Dionysus*, commissioned for Brookgreen Gardens in 1936, displays a cool reserve in composition enhanced by rhythmic curves providing balance and harmony.

The elegant figure of *Diana* presents McCartan's mature style. A critic wrote of this work: "He is a child of Houdon, say, simply in that it is natural to him to compose in terms of an animated mundane elegance and to stress in his figures the precious quality of line. The *Diana* is perhaps his outstanding triumph in this regard. Its contours have a delectably pure and flowing linear distinction. How spare and refined the lovely figure is!"

SOURCES:
Cortissoz, Royal, "The Sculpture of Edward McCartan,"
   Scribner's Magazine 83 (February 1928): 243.
Proske, Beatrice Gilman, *Brookgreen Gardens Sculpture*
   (Murrells Inlet, S.C.: Brookgreen Gardens, 1968) 221-223.

Diana
Bronze, 1922
23 x 20 x 12 in. (58.4 x 50.8 x 30.5 cm.)
Signed: *E· MC CARTAN 19 © 22 N°. 2*

Richard McDermott Miller

Born 1922, New Philadelphia, Ohio

The powerful figures of Richard Miller set his work apart from that of his contemporaries. They are designed not only for the presentation of subject, but for the handling of surrounding space.

Miller was one of the first sculptors to set up a studio in New York City's SoHo district. Though he had created sculpture from the age of ten and his work won awards at the Cleveland Institute of Art, he did not become a full-time sculptor until the age of forty. Working directly from life, Miller models figures in wax and clay to be cast in bronze. While the monumental figure has been a specialty, his work also includes smaller designs. Movement is an important part of his sculpture. This feeling for mass and contour gives his female figures exceptional sensuality.

Wind on the Water is a prime example of his sense of design. The balance of billowing drapery in counterpoise to forward movement presents an unique composition.

He is a successful teacher who has authored several books on sculpture technique. Miller has stated his personal philosophy: "Only by doing sculpture does one become a sculptor. Only by involving ourselves in actual working problems can we begin to translate our insights and feelings into sculptural terms. And only through such development, can we begin to find in our work a form of personal expression which is uniquely our own."

SOURCES:
Miller, Richard McDermott, *Figure Sculpture in Wax and Plaster* (New York: Watson-Guptill Publications, 1971; New York: Dover Publications, Inc., 1987).
Miller, Richard McDermott, *Richard McDermott Miller, The Figure Sculptor of Soho* (New York: privately printed, 1981) [brochure].

Wind on the Water
Bronze, 1992
103 x 92 in. (261.6 x 233.6 cm.)
Signed: *RICHARD McDERMOTT MILLER*
Gift of the sculptor
(Shown at Brookgreen Gardens only; represented by a photo mural in the traveling exhibition.)

Carl Wilhelm Andersson Milles

Born 1875, near Uppsala, Sweden
Died 1955, Lidingo, Sweden

Marked by an impish sense of humor and love of satire, Carl Milles's philosophy was presented in sculpture that speaks of human warmth and spiritual hope. The combination of water and movement, key to his work's expression, earned Milles recognition as the greatest twentieth-century sculptor of fountains. Although he did not come to America until the age of fifty-nine, he was an important influence in American art through his position as resident sculptor at the Cranbrook Academy of Art.

At the age of seventeen, Milles was apprenticed to a cabinetmaker and studied woodworking, carving and modeling in evening classes in Stockholm. In 1897, while en route to a job in Chile, he stopped in Paris and, entranced by its artistic atmosphere, decided to stay. Supporting himself as a cabinetmaker and ornament molder, he attended lectures at the Académie Colarossi and classes at the École des Beaux-Arts. Milles became attracted by the decorative elements in the work of Dalou and Falguière and was influenced by Maillol and Bourdelle. He frequented the studio of Auguste Rodin, where he worked for a while as an assistant. During this period his figures became stylized and elongated with an emphasis on upward movement.

By 1906 Milles was receiving prestigious commissions in his native country, yet his singular style in sculpture frequently ran against the prevailing taste and was often criticized. After enjoying a brief period of acceptance in 1914, by 1917 Milles was so dissatisfied that he destroyed most of the models in his studio. From this point he entered a period of rapid stylistic development which included the use of granite as a medium. Within five years, at the age of fifty, Milles was again receiving acclaim for his sculpture. In 1927, an international career was launched with an exhibition at the Tate Gallery in London, the first showing of his work outside of Sweden.

In 1929, Milles made his first trip to America, where he visited fellow Scandinavian Eliel Saarinen, director of the Cranbrook Academy of Art in Bloomfield Hills, Michigan. Two years later, Milles was appointed resident sculptor and head of the sculpture department, a position he held for twenty years. In 1934, the Cranbrook Foundation acquired an impressive collection of his sculpture. Through the 1930s, his work traveled to exhibitions in Saint Louis, Chicago, Cleveland, Detroit and New York — cities which became permanent locations for his major fountain sculptures including *The Triton Fountain, Meeting of the Waters* and *Man and Nature*.

The Fountain of the Muses, consisting of eight major figures and seven secondary ones, was modeled in a studio at the American Academy in Rome. The work was commissioned by the trustees of The Metropolitan Museum of Art in 1949 and casting of the figures was completed just six months before Milles's death, in 1955. This final work depicts the Greek myth of the fountain sacred to the muses. The male figures, representing poetry, architecture, music, painting and sculpture, have just sipped the fountain's inspirational waters. On the pool's edge are a centaur, faun and a female figure representing the nine muses. The group was purchased from The Metropolitan Museum of Art in 1982. Castings of four of the large figures are exhibited at Millesgarden, the sculptor's home and studio, now a museum near Stockholm.

SOURCES:
Arvidsson, Karl Axel, ed., *Carl Milles, Episodes from my Life* (Stockholm, Sweden: Millesgarden and Ehrenblad Editions AB, 1991).
Jones, Virgil, "Milles: Whimsical, Controversial, Great," *National Sculpture Review* (Winter 1985-86).
Rogers, Meyric R., *Carl Milles, An Interpretation of his Work* (New Haven: Yale University Press, 1940).
Taylor, Francis Henry, "Aganippe: The Fountain of the Muses," *The Metropolitan Museum of Art Bulletin*, 14, No. 5, (1956).

The Fountain of the Muses
Bronze, 1949-1955
Life-size figures, fifteen piece fountain group
(Represented by a photo mural.)

Elie Nadelman

Born 1882, Warsaw, Poland
Died 1946, Riverdale, New York

Elie Nadelman studied art in Warsaw and Krakow, then in 1904 went to Munich for six months and on to Paris. While visiting Munich's museums, opera halls and circus, Nadelman came under the influence of a range of art and decorative works, including classic Greek sculptures and antique dolls. In Paris he took a studio and began to make drawings after works by Michelangelo that he saw at the Louvre, and felt the influence of Seurat and Rodin. But the emotionalism of Rodin's art did not manifest itself in Nadelman's artistic vision. Some of his drawings were exhibited in the Salon d'Automne from 1905 to 1907. Leo Stein, in the company of Picasso, came to Nadelman's studio in 1908 and purchased several drawings and a sculpture in plaster. The following year, the sculptor's first solo exhibition met with great success at the Galerie Druet.

By 1910, his personal statement of abstraction was published in *Camera Work*. Nadelman thought of himself as the first proponent of cubism in sculpture, and, in 1925, wrote an article asserting the importance of his influence. Four years earlier he had written in the preface to his own publication of a series of drawings that *Recherches de formes et de volumes,* "...introduced into painting and sculpture abstract form until then wholly lacking. Cubism was only an imitation of the abstract forms of these drawings and did not attain their plastic significance." In fact, he dated his experiments in cubism as far back as 1905, when geometric form began to show in his drawings. It is almost certain that Picasso was influenced by his visit to Nadelman's studio in 1908.

An entire exhibition of his work in 1911 at Paterson's Gallery in London was purchased by Helena Rubinstein, launching a relationship based on business and friendship. At the beginning of World War I, with her assistance, Nadelman obtained passage to the United States. With Rubinstein's patronage and Lincoln Kirstein's promotion, Nadelman's work began to attract serious collectors. Within a year after arriving in New York, one of his ideal heads, carved in marble, entered the collection of the Rhode Island School of Design. These works of plaster, wood and marble, having classical antecedents, yet utilizing an entirely different way of handling mass, had no precedent in American art. Polished to a porcelain-like finish, the smooth surfaces were enhanced by the brilliant effect. In some examples, the simplified forms were highly mannered images of serenity; in others, a spherical construction in relation to the eyes, cheeks and forehead had no relation to classicism. In their evolution can be traced Nadelman's stylistic growth.

After marriage in 1919, Nadelman and his wife began to collect folk art and eventually built a museum to house the collection on the grounds of their estate at Riverdale, New York. Unfortunately, after the effects of the Great Depression, Nadelman had to sell off the art in order to live. The influences of folk art on his sculpture are evident in such works as *Host* and *La Femme Assise,* two painted cherrywood carvings that were reduced to simple, rounded forms, like naive caricatures. Later in his career he began to work in terra cotta and papier-mâché, creating figurines that could be mass-produced for homes. In these works, many of which were left in his studio at his death, he tried to achieve a monumental feeling, scaled down to a convenient household size.

A synthesis of folk, classical and modern influences, Nadelman's composition, like his drawing, was based on a succession of curves. A series of animals done in the years immediately following his arrival in New York, present the elegant smoothness of contour that made him known as "poet of the plastic curve." *Resting Stag's* simple geometric line is a fine example of the innovative and imaginative quality of his work. Its beauty is enhanced by the sleekly rounded masses of the animal's body in contrast to the slender legs and antlers.

SOURCES:
Baur, John I. H., *The Sculpture and Drawings of Elie Nadelman* (New York: Whitney Museum of American Art, 1975).
Birnbaum, Martin, "Elie Nadelman," *International Studio* (December 1915): 53-55.
Kramer, Hilton, "For Nadelman, There Is No Lost Grandeur," *The New York Times* (17 March 1974): Art Section, 27.
Nadelman, Elie, *Vers la beauté plastique: thirty-two reproductions of drawings* (New York: privately published, 1921).
Proske, Beatrice Gilman, *Brookgreen Gardens Sculpture* (Murrells Inlet, S.C.: Brookgreen Gardens, 1968) 278-280.

Resting Stag
Bronze, c. 1917
16.5 x 21 x 8 in. (41.9 x 53.3 x 20.3 cm.)

Charles Cropper Parks

Born 1922, Onancock, Virginia

The sculpture of Charles Parks is as diverse as his methods and materials. Simple acts and pleasures of life, such as a girl combing her hair and a child holding a rabbit, are modeled with sensitivity and warmth. His fresh approach and mastery of portraiture is especially evident in works of children. Parks, who came to sculpture as a full–time profession later in life, worked for many years in his family's machine tool business. There he acquired a solid mechanical background that has enabled him to develop innovative sculpture techniques that are uniquely his own.

The period of the 1960s marked the onset of sculpture as a full-time career. Experimentation with non-traditional materials and design resulted in works like nothing he had previously done. The Brittingham Arts Foundation Award in 1961 allowed him to study the new media and techniques made available by technology. His previous welding experience inspired the medium of choice for a number of corten steel sculptures and reliefs. Even with the challenge of new materials, he continued to create other, more traditional works intended for bronze.

A travel grant from the Wemys Foundation in 1965 allowed Parks to spend a year studying and working in Greece. There he experimented with wrought iron and stone, immersing himself in the artistic tradition of the Mediterranean. Influences from this period appear in the strong, spare line of his works with religious themes and in sculpture with richly modeled detail. The wool of *Aries,* a life-size bronze ram done in 1966, is patterned in precise curls similar to the treatment of fur in archaic Greek sculpture.

Also in the 1960s, Parks began to work in portraiture, a format to which he is particularly suited. His subjects, characteristically informally clothed and posed, vary widely in age and background. But, it is in sculpture of children that Charles Parks finds a special affinity. He translates the essence of the sitter to heads, busts and figures projecting the innocence and inquisitiveness of youth. The life-size works, presented in casual settings with the subject's favorite pets or playthings, combine portraiture and outdoor sculpture in a pleasing manner.

A strong religious belief underlies Parks's philosophy of art and its place in the world. His concern for and empathy with his fellow man has formed the basis for works of a social nature. Avoiding stereotypes, Parks has depicted the themes of old age, childhood, the traditional family and family roles in a number of public pieces designed as monuments and fountains. In the early 1960s, he developed a method to enlarge and weld steel from a small model. This technique, perfected through years of work, is exemplified by *Our Lady of Peace,* the largest sculpture of its type. In it, stainless steel strips are painstakingly welded piece by piece to create a smoothly flowing effect, quite different from his earlier welded forms.

Parks's ability to convey emotion in his sculpture and to set a mood for the viewer has brought him important awards and commissions. *Long Long Thoughts* won the Gold Medal at the Grand National Exhibition of the American Artists Professional League in 1971. Originally a commissioned portrait, the positive public response to this sculpture convinced the owner to allow the sculptor to cast it in an edition of twenty–five. The title was taken from a verse by Longfellow: "A boy's will is the wind's will, And the thoughts of youth are long, long thoughts." The sculptor wrote of it, "There is something serious and profound in every child...a sort of inner being."

SOURCES:
Craven, Wayne, "Charles Parks – A Biography Midway," *National Sculpture Review* (Spring 1972) 16-17, 28-29.
Mahr, Nancy, "The Parks Family: Where Extraordinary is the Norm," *Delaware Today* (September 1971) 11-13, 42-47.

Long Long Thoughts
Bronze, 1972
24.5 x 14 x 14 in. (62.2 x 35.6 x 35.6 cm.)
Signed: *PARKS* © 5

Hiram Powers

Born 1805, Woodstock, Vermont
Died 1873, Florence, Italy

The most noted sculptor of his day, Hiram Powers owed much to the support of wealthy patrons — especially Nicholas Longworth of Ohio and John Preston of South Carolina. Powers settled in Florence, Italy, in the late 1830s and remained there for the rest of his life, making only one return trip to America. He was one of many expatriate Americans who were attracted to Florence for its less restrictive government allowing greater creative expression. Although surrounded by the art of antiquity, Powers did not travel widely on the continent. His sculpture, as a result, was not greatly influenced by European art and remained distinctly American.

While *The Greek Slave,* his most famous work, was being cut in marble, Powers was creating a model of a sculpture for Hamilton Fish of New York. The artist wrote, "It represents a lad of thirteen years holding a conch shell to his ear with one hand, while in the other is held a fishing net and a boat tiller. He is listening to the sound of the sea, believing that the shell has the power to warn him of the weather."

Powers drew upon Italian folklore as a device to allow him to portray a naked youth. Although *The Fisher Boy,* Powers' only treatment of the male nude, would have been uncontroversial in Italy, it required the literary context to be accepted in America. The shell was copied from an example borrowed from the Grand Ducal Cabinet in Florence. Only six examples of *The Fisher Boy* were carved. This example was purchased by Robert Stephenson of Newcastle-Upon-Tyne, England, in November 1845 and remained in his family until acquired by Brookgreen Gardens.

SOURCES:
Crane, Sylvia, *White Silence: Greenough, Powers and Crawford, American Sculptors in Nineteenth-Century Italy* (Coral Gables, Fla.: University of Miami Press, 1972).
Reynolds, Donald M., *Hiram Powers and His Ideal Sculpture* (New York: Garland, 1977).
Thorp, Margaret Farrand, *The Literary Sculptors* (Durham, N.C.: Duke University Press, 1965).
Wunder, Richard P., *Hiram Powers,* Vol. 1 and 2 (Newark, Del.: University of Delware Press, 1991).

The Fisher Boy
White marble, 1846
Height: 57 in. (144.8 cm.)
Signed: *H.POWERS Sculp. 1846*

Brenda Putnam

Born 1890, Minneapolis, Minnesota
Died 1975, Concord, New Hampshire

Brenda Putnam did not lack for stimulating surroundings. Her grandfather was publisher George P. Putnam; her father, Herbert Putnam, was for many years Librarian of Congress; and her brother was married to Amelia Earhart. Putnam began art study at the age of fifteen in Boston with Bela Pratt. Later, she studied modeling with James Earle Fraser at the Art Students League and portrait sculpture with Charles Grafly.

Her early work, influenced by Renaissance art, featured merry children in a series of sundials, fountains and reliefs. She also specialized in bas-relief portraits of children. An interest in music resulted in a series of portraits of musicians including Pablo Casals. During the 1920s, Putnam shared a studio in New York with the sculptor Anna Hyatt and violinist Edith Rubel.

Public commissions included a mischievous *Puck* for the Folger Shakespeare Library at Washington, D.C., a memorial to the women of Virginia for Spring Hill Cemetery at Lynchburg and her last sculpture, a bust of Susan B. Anthony for the Hall of Fame at New York University. Putnam wrote two books on sculpture technique, *The Sculptor's Way, A Guide to Modeling and Sculpture* and *Animal X-Rays: A Skeleton Key to Comparative Anatomy.*

After 1927 as she investigated the cubism theories of Archipenko and studied in Florence with Libero Andreotti, her sculpture became more streamlined in keeping with the art deco style. Despite this move away from realistic detail, her work continued to exude life and warmth. This is evident in *Communion,* the sympathetic portrait of Mary Baillie, whom Putnam portrayed with tenderness and dignity. Mother of a prominent stone carver, she was well known by the sculptors who employed her son.

In *The Sculptor's Way,* Putnam summarized her philosophy for the student, "If the sculptor is to speak to more than just a handful of his brethren, he must enlarge his horizon. If the sculptor is again to lead us to the heights, he must be broadly human....The sculptor, as poet, must have a wide vocabulary to choose from if he hopes to find the significant words that will attract and hold the attention of his hearers. He must have a mastery of form, an innate sense of rhythm, an ability to vitalize the telling of his own thought or emotion so that his reader lives it with him. His imagery must be vivid, his climax forceful, his subtle allusions full of infinite suggestion."

SOURCES:
Proske, Beatrice Gilman, *Brookgreen Gardens Sculpture* (Murrells Inlet, S.C.: Brookgreen Gardens, 1968) 244-248.
Putnam, Brenda, *The Sculptor's Way, A Guide to Modeling and Sculpture* (New York: Watson Guptill Publications, Inc., 1948) 19-20.
Rubinstein, Charlotte Streifer, *American Women Sculptors: A History of Women Working in Three Dimensions* (Boston: G. K. Hall & Co., 1990) 248-249.

Communion
Bronze, 1939
52 x 24 x 24 in. (132.1 x 60.9 x 60.9 cm.)
Signed: *BRENDA PUTNAM 1939*

Frederic Sackrider Remington

Born 1861, Canton, New York
Died 1909, Ridgefield, Connecticut

An acclaimed illustrator of western life, Frederic Remington moved easily into the field of sculpture. His work chronicled the events and attitudes of America's western movement, as seen from the viewpoint of settlers, soldiers and cowboys. These scenes, rendered in pen and ink drawings, black and white washes and oil paintings, captured the rough spirit of the people of the plains. Most of his art includes horses in the composition, to such an extent that he chose for his epitaph the lines, "He knew the horse."

The Bronco Buster, Remington's first attempt in bronze, was difficult enough technically to daunt an experienced sculptor. Characteristic of the artist, he forged ahead and the sculpture was an immediate success. The asymmetric design and violent movement apparent in the horse and rider not only set a new standard for technical ability, but opened the field of Western art as a new market. The earliest versions were sandcast at the Henry-Bonnard Foundry. Around 1900, Remington moved his models to Roman Bronze Works, where the lost-wax process gave him greater flexibility in the creation of his sculptures. Remington made continual small changes in the composition and refinements in the modeling. This example, which eliminated some details and has smoother modeling, is a later version, cast by Roman Bronze Works.

Although he created only a few pieces of sculpture, in comparison to the number of commissions received by his contemporaries, his contribution to American art was significant. *The Bronco Buster,* with more than 300 castings, is the largest known edition of American bronze sculpture. Frederic Remington died at the age of forty-eight, cutting short a life of creative vitality.

SOURCES:
Proske, Beatrice Gilman, *Brookgreen Gardens Sculpture* (Murrells Inlet, S.C.: Brookgreen Gardens, 1968) 66-69.
Shapiro, Michael Edward, *Bronze Casting and American Sculpture 1850-1900* (Newark: University of Delaware Press, 1985).

The Bronco Buster
Bronze, c. 1895
23.5 x 15 x 7.5 in. (59.7 x 38.1 x 19 cm.)
Signed: *Frederic Remington*

Augustus Saint-Gaudens

Born 1848, Dublin, Ireland
Died 1907, Cornish, New Hampshire

Augustus Saint-Gaudens was a major artistic influence in late nineteenth–century America. His innovative composition and inspired technique brought him acclaim and success. As a creator and mentor, Saint-Gaudens presided over the rise of American sculpture and promoted its advancement.

During his student days in New York City at the Cooper Union and the National Academy of Design school, an apprenticeship with a cameocutter provided a source of income. At the age of nineteen Saint-Gaudens went to Paris, where he studied with Jouffroy and became associated with Falguière and Mercié. A fascination with the Renaissance led him to Rome, where he studied the art and techniques that would establish his future eminence in relief sculpture and medallic art.

Upon returning to New York, in 1875, he established a studio and developed a working relationship with the painter John LaFarge and the architect Stanford White. This collaboration led to several works, including Saint-Gaudens's first major commission, a statue of Admiral Farragut for Madison Square in New York City. His innovative design and meticulous craftsmanship set new standards for excellence in bas-relief and monumental sculpture. Saint-Gaudens's fertile imagination expressed itself in sculpture that combined a spiritual quality and romantic interpretation, marking a break with Neoclassicism and the beginning of a new American style.

The Puritan, first done in 1887 to commemorate Deacon Samuel Chapin, a founder of Springfield, Massachusetts, is a good example of Saint-Gaudens's groundbreaking work. He remodeled his initial composition, rearranging and repeating the folds of the cloak, and placing the figure in different positions, until he was satisfied with the design. The individuality of *The Puritan* was the result of the informal pose — the stern figure boldly striding toward the viewer — and the period costume with walking stick, that enhances the figure's personal quality.

SOURCES:
Dryfhout, John H., *The Work of Augustus Saint-Gaudens* (Hanover and London: University Press of New England, 1982).
Greenthal, Kathryn, *Augustus Saint-Gaudens, Master Sculptor* (New York: The Metropolitan Museum of Art, 1985).

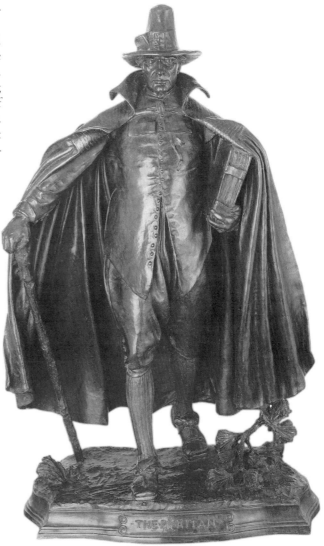

The Puritan
Bronze, 1887
30.5 x 10 x 10 in. (77.5 x 25.4 x 25.4 cm.)
Signed: *AVGVSTVS · SAINT GAUDENS*
Front: · *THE PVRITAN* ·

Janet (Netta Deweze Frazee) Scudder

Born 1873, Terre Haute, Indiana
Died 1940, Rockport, Massachusetts

One of the greatest American sculptors of works for the garden, Janet Scudder, attained her renown through great personal tenacity and struggle. After assisting Lorado Taft as one of the White Rabbits, a group of women sculptors hired to complete the building ornamentation and enlargements of outdoor sculpture at the World's Columbian Exposition in 1893, Scudder was ready to find her special niche. Her work for the Exposition earned a bronze medal — the first of many honors.

Impressed by the exuberance of Frederick MacMonnies' work for the Exposition, Scudder went to Paris with Zulime Taft, Lorado Taft's artist sister, hoping to persuade MacMonnies to accept her as a student. She was turned away several times before he finally agreed and took her on as a worker in his studio. During this three-year period, she also studied at the Académie Colarossi.

On a subsequent trip in Italy, the sculpture of the Renaissance inspired her vision. After her return to Paris, a street urchin captivated her with his frivolity, as he danced about her studio. She wrote, "In that moment a finished work flashed before me. I saw a little boy dancing, laughing, chuckling all to himself while a spray of water dashed over him. The idea of my Frog Fountain was born." The result

of that encounter was the sculpture *Frog Baby*. Also life-size, it launched the series of fountains for which she is best known. Of the four life-size examples, two were sold to Stanford White for his clients, introducing her work to an ever-widening circle of patrons.

SOURCES:
Hall, Alice, "Fountains Designed by Janet Scudder," *The House Beautiful* 36 (June 1914): 10-12.
McSpadden, J. Walker, *Famous Sculptors of America* (Freeport, N.Y.: Books for Libraries Press, 1924; reprint 1968).
Mechlin, Leila, "Janet Scudder—Sculptor," *The International Studio* 39 (February 1910) 81-88.
Scudder, Janet, *Modeling My Life* (New York: Harcourt, Brace & Co., 1925).
Warlick, Mary E., "Janet Scudder...Pioneer in Garden Sculpture," *National Sculpture Review* (1977): 14-17.

Frog Baby
Bronze, 1901
12.25 x 3 x 3 in. (31.1 x 7.6 x 7.6 cm.)
Signed: *JANET SCUDDER*

Lorado Taft

Born 1860, Elmwood, Illinois
Died 1936, Chicago, Illinois

Lorado Taft made Chicago a focus for American sculpture. Among the first to evolve a monumental style, Taft lectured on art history at the Universities of Chicago and Illinois, and wrote the first comprehensive survey of American sculpture. For a twenty-year period he also taught modeling at the Art Institute and many American sculptors in the late nineteenth and early twentieth centuries began their studies with him.

In 1880, Taft left Chicago to study sculpture in Paris. At the École des Beaux-Arts he received instruction from Augustin Dumont, Jean Bonnassieux and Jules Thomas over a five-year period. He also worked briefly for Injalbert and received criticisms from Mercié. In 1886, he returned to Chicago after receiving a commission for a monument to an Indiana statesman. It was the World's Columbian Exposition held in Chicago in 1893 that brought Taft's work to the fore. He received recognition with two groups for the Horticulture Building, — *The Sleep of the Flowers* and *The Awakening of the Flowers.* He also achieved a prominent position in art history by hiring a number of women sculptors to help him complete his work under deadline. They became known as the White Rabbits, after he was told that he could hire anyone to help — white rabbits, if they would do the work. The group of women included Enid Yandell, who went on to study with Rodin; Janet Scudder, who made a name for herself in the field of garden sculpture; and Evelyn Longman, the only woman ever allowed to work in the studio of Daniel Chester French.

Taft's preference for large-scale works manifested itself in a series of monumental fountains. *Fountain of the Great Lakes,* completed in 1913, was a group of five female figures pouring water from shells. *The Fountain of Time* and *Fountain of Creation* were part of an elaborate plan for sculptural ornamentation of Midway, Washington and Jackson Parks in Chicago. Taft was most satisfied when he could release imaginative flights of fancy in composition and symbolism. In *The Fountain of Time,* a procession of human forms are arranged in a wave pattern before a solitary figure representing Time. The theme was inspired by lines of Henry Austin Dobson

from The *Paradox of Time*: "Time goes, you say? Ah no! Alas, Time stays, we go." He experimented with concrete as a sculpture medium for this work.

Daughter of Pyrrha refers to the myth of Deucalion and Pyrrha, the evolution of man from matter, in stones taking human shape. It is a study for one of the figures in the *Fountain of Creation,* a work left unfinished at Taft's death. Just becoming aware of her existence, she expresses a rise to consciousness from nascency to full awareness. In the overall work, a ring of figures emerges from stone, each figure progressively becoming more completely formed and rising higher. Water was to flow among the groups of figures. The working model of *Daughter of Pyrrha* was made and exhibited in 1910, but was not cast until 1934, when it was acquired by Brookgreen Gardens. Taft's intention was to have the completed fountain placed at the east end of the Midway, opposite the *Fountain of Time.* When he died nearly all of the small working models were finished, fourteen were enlarged in plaster and four, including this one, were carved in limestone. The four completed figures were left along with the contents of his studio to the University of Illinois.

SOURCES:
Browne, Charles Francis, "Lorado Taft: Sculptor," *The World To-day* 14 (February 1908): 191-198.
Clark, Neil M., "A Wonderful Thing Happened to this Boy!" *The American Magazine* 93 (April 1922).
Proske, Beatrice Gilman, *Brookgreen Gardens Sculpture* (Murrells Inlet, S.C.: Brookgreen Gardens, 1968) 41-44.
Taft, Lorado, *Modern Tendencies in Sculpture* (Chicago: University of Chicago Press, 1921).
Weller, Allen Stuart, *Lorado in Paris: The Letters of Lorado Taft, 1880-1885* (Urbana and Chicago: University of Illinois Press, 1985).

Daughter of Pyrrha
Bronze, c. 1909
12 x 4 x 6 in. (30.5 x 10.1 x 15.2 cm.)
Signed: *Lorado Taft. Sc.*

John Quincy Adams Ward

Born 1830, Urbana, Ohio
Died 1910, New York City

Ward's credo — to depict American themes with a simple, direct naturalism — earned him a prominent position in nineteenth-century art history. The use of natural poses and richly textured surfaces characterized his works.

After seven years of study with Henry Kirke Brown and assisting in his Brooklyn studio, Ward began to work on his own, modeling portrait busts in Washington, D.C., and in Columbus, Ohio. It is significant that he never studied in Europe. Early on he developed the belief that American artists should portray native ideals and that opportunities should be made for artists to learn craftsmanship in this country. His artistry was developed through technical experimentation and perseverance.

Ward returned to New York in 1861 and took a foundry job designing decorative objects such as handles for military presentation swords. Later commissions for monuments to public figures, such as *Horace Greeley* at New York and *Henry Ward Beecher* at Brooklyn, allowed him to concentrate on the character of the individual, rather than on the decorative value of the work. Presented in everyday clothes with personal attributes intact, these figures gained Ward widespread recognition for their simplicity and dignity.

The Indian Hunter, a powerful influence on the sculptors who followed, brought Ward critical acclaim for its lifelike treatment. Initially modeled in 1857, Ward enlarged and reworked the design in 1864, after a trip to study Native Americans of the Northwest. The hunter in the second version has a more ethnic appearance and the hide upon the ground is removed. After enthusiastic public response at a New York gallery exhibition, *The Indian Hunter* was one of the first pieces placed in Central Park, New York City. A cast of this sculpture also marks Ward's grave at Urbana, Ohio.

As the leader of the group of post-Civil War realists, Ward played a major role in the advancement of American sculpture. Active until the end of his life, he continued to be involved in the evolution of American art and provided encouragement to a new generation of sculptors.

SOURCES:
McSpadden, J. Walker, *Famous Sculptors of America* (Freeport, N.Y.: Books for Libraries Press, 1924; reprint, 1968).
Proske, Beatrice Gilman, *Brookgreen Gardens Sculpture* (Murrells Inlet, S.C., Brookgreen Gardens, 1968) 3-7.
Sharp, Lewis I., *John Quincy Adams Ward, Dean of American Sculpture* (Newark: University of Delaware Press, 1985).

The Indian Hunter
Bronze, c. 1857
15.75 x 14.25 x 8.25 in. (40 x 36.2 x 21 cm.)
Signed: *J. Q. A. WARD 1860*

Katharine Ward Lane Weems

Born 1899, Boston, Massachusetts
Died 1989, Manchester, Massachusetts

A member of a wealthy Boston family, Katharine Lane was encouraged to pursue an artistic career by Anna Hyatt. Hyatt's studio at Seven Acres, the family farm at Annisquam, Massachusetts, was a favorite haunt for Lane, when her family spent time at their summer home in nearby Manchester. Although not enthusiastic over the young artist's career choice, Lane's family allowed her to study in Boston, at the school of the Museum of Fine Arts, where her father served on the board of trustees. She received additional instruction from Charles Grafly and from Brenda Putnam, who shared a New York studio with Hyatt.

Making animal sculpture in bronze her specialty, Lane portrayed greyhounds, whippets, horses and exotic animals. Each subject is invested with a particular personality. Her early work displayed her flair for design; later pieces were simplified without sacrificing detail. Her work was not limited to small bronzes, however. Utilizing a technique based on Chinese tomb carvings of the Han Period, Lane completed a commission in 1933 for three friezes carved directly into the brick of the Biological Laboratories at Harvard University. Later, for the same building, she completed decorative doors featuring a variety of insects and modeled a pair of Indian rhinoceros for the entrance.

Her animal sculpture won prizes from the National Sculpture Society, the Pennsylvania Academy of the Fine Arts, The National Arts Club and the National Academy of Design, as both her artistic output and talent grew unabated. Criticism and encouragement in the early years from mentors Hyatt and Putnam came full circle when *April,* a study of a small goat, received the Anna Hyatt Huntington Prize of the National Association of Women Artists in 1931. After her marriage in 1947, to longtime friend F. Carrington Weems, she divided her time between New York City and Manchester, Massachusetts.

Greyhounds Unleashed, a pair of greyhounds racing side by side, is an example of Weems's eye for composition and distinctive style. The canine lean nervousness and rapid forward movement are elegantly and gracefully depicted.

SOURCES:
Ambler, Louise Todd, *Katharine Lane Weems, Sculpture and Drawings* (Boston: The Boston Athenaeum, 1987).
Proske, Beatrice Gilman, *Brookgreen Gardens Sculpture* (Murrells Inlet, S.C.: Brookgreen Gardens, 1968) 405-408.
Weems, Katharine Lane, as told to Edward Weeks, *Odds Were Against Me* (New York: Vantage Press, 1985).

Greyhounds Unleashed
Bronze, c. 1928
10 x 15.5 x 7 in.
(25.4 x 39.3 x 17.7 cm.)
Signed: *KATHARINE W. LANE. ~ 1928 ~ ©*

Adolph Alexander Weinman

Born 1870, Karlsruhe, Germany
Died 1952, Port Chester, New York

Exquisite modeling and refined technique mark the work of German-born sculptor, A. A. Weinman. His skill was honed through study at Cooper Union and the Art Students League and apprenticeship to a carver of wood and ivory. Weinman went on to work in the studios of Philip Martiny, Olin Warner, Augustus Saint-Gaudens, Charles Niehaus and Daniel Chester French, before opening his own studio in 1904.

Although best known for architectural sculpture, including decorative panels for the Morgan Library in New York City, pediments for the capitols of Wisconsin and Missouri, and friezes for many of the neoclassical buildings of Washington, D.C., Weinman created a wide range of award-winning artworks. The play of light and shadow over his sculpture was often a major part of the design. His feeling for line and pattern gave his work movement and enabled him to present mass in perfect balance. Weinman's creation of *Riders of the Dawn,* commissioned by Archer Huntington for Brookgreen Gardens in 1941, displays this powerful ability to its greatest extent. The pair of riders on stallions rearing from the depths of the ocean are good examples of harmonious pattern and dynamic movement.

Weinman's mastery extended to the field of medallic art, where his skillful composition produced everything from relief portraits of children to the country's coinage, including the Liberty Head dime and the 1916 half dollar. In 1920, the American Numismatic Society awarded him the J. Sanford Saltus Medal for lifetime achievement in medallic art. The Saltus Medal was one which Weinman had designed.

The delightful composition of *Duet,* with the young faun mirroring the action of the older satyr, is Weinman at his best. The design, reminiscent of oriental art, is carried out with masterful detail. Beautiful from all perspectives, this work is made more intricate by the use of the twisted oak branch, which draws the viewer's eye around the piece.

SOURCES:
Proske, Beatrice Gilman, *Brookgreen Gardens Sculpture* (Murrells Inlet, S.C.: Brookgreen Gardens, 1968) 120-125.

Duet
Bronze, 1924
24 x 19.5 x 12 in. (60.9 x 49.5 x 30.5 cm.)
Signed: *A · A · WEINMAN · SC 19 © 24*

Gertrude Vanderbilt Whitney

Born 1877, New York City
Died 1942, New York City

Born to wealth and privilege, Gertrude Vanderbilt struggled with her family to be allowed to pursue sculpturing and with fellow artists to take her commitment to art seriously. After her marriage to Harry Payne Whitney in 1896, she studied with Hendrick Andersen and James Earle Fraser. Additional instruction was received at the Art Students League, and in Paris, where she entered the studio of Andrew O'Connor. From him she developed a fluid technique of modeling, with vaguely defined masses reminiscent of Rodin, O'Connor's teacher.

The *Titanic Memorial* at Washington, D.C., one of her best known public works, was also her first commission won in competition. A lone figure with arms spread in the shape of a cross represents the sacrifice of the individuals who died with the sinking of the ocean liner. As a prominent philanthropist, she provided funds for struggling and out of work artists during the depression years. Gertrude Vanderbilt Whitney aided fellow artists by establishing the Whitney Studio Club in her Macdougall Alley studio in 1914. Here artists could create their works and have a place to exhibit. She also purchased art, gathering a collection of contemporary paintings and sculpture, that evolved into the Whitney Museum of American Art, founded in 1930.

Caryatid is a sketch for one of the figures in a marble fountain presented to McGill University, Montreal, in 1931, as a symbol of international good will. The fountain was originally modeled for the Arlington Hotel in Washington, D.C.. The three caryatid figures support a large basin upon their heads, forming a tripod-like pedestal over which water pours, spilling into a catch basin at their feet. In 1913, it was awarded honorable mention at the Paris Salon and received the National Arts Club Prize of the National Association of Women

Painters and Sculptors in 1914. A bronze version of the fountain is in Lima, Peru, and castings of the single *Caryatid* are also in the collections of the Whitney Museum of American Art and The Metropolitan Museum of Art.

SOURCES:
Friedman, B. H., *Gertrude Vanderbilt Whitney* (Garden City, New York: Doubleday & Company, Inc., 1978).
Proske, Beatrice Gilman, *Brookgreen Gardens Sculpture* (Murrells Inlet, S.C.: Brookgreen Gardens, 1968) 206-208.

Caryatid
Bronze, 1913
23 x 5 x 5 in. (58.4 x 12.7 x 12.7 cm.)
Signed: *Gertrude V. Whitney 1913*

Acknowledgements

The Brookgreen Gardens Board of Trustees and Lawrence Henry, President and CEO, deserve recognition for their vision in revising the collections policy to allow temporary indoor exhibitions and the travel of Brookgreen's collections. Without their support and cooperation, this project would not have been possible.

The exhibition at Brookgreen Gardens is sponsored by a generous donation from the BMW Manufacturing Corp., marking the first sponsorship by BMW of a major museum exhibition in America. Special appreciation is reserved for Helmut Panke, Chairman and CEO of BMW Holding Corp.; Carl Flesher, Vice President of Corporate and Community Relations, BMW Manufacturing Corp.; and the Honorable Carroll A. Campbell, Jr., Brookgreen Trustee and former Governor of South Carolina, for their dedication to this achievement.

Conservation of the sculpture in the exhibition was carried out by Theodore Monnich, Chief Conservator of the South Carolina State Museum. A portion of this project was funded by a grant from the South Carolina Arts Commission, which receives support from the National Endowment for the Arts.

Sincere thanks are extended to Ilene Susan Fort, Curator of American Art, Los Angeles County Museum of Art, and to Lauretta Dimmick, Gates Curator of Paintings and Sculpture, Denver Art Museum, for their excellent essays. Since both of these scholars are in constant demand, their efforts in support of this project are greatly appreciated.

The assistance of colleagues in other organizations who provided information and visual materials from their collections, is greatly appreciated: Wanda Styka, Chesterwood, a museum property of the National Trust for Historic Preservation, Stockbridge, Massachusetts; Cynthia Mathews, Chicago Historical Society, Chicago, Illinois; Library of Congress, Washington, D.C.; Ingrid Steiner, Maier Museum of Art, Randolph-Macon Woman's College, Lynchburg, Virginia; David Dearinger, National Academy of Design, New York City; Joan Stahl, Andrew Thomas, National Museum of American Art, Peter A. Juley & Son Collection, Washington, D.C.; Joanna Britto, Ann Shumard, National Portrait Gallery, Washington, D.C.; Gwen Pier, National Sculpture Society, New York City; Brenda Wetzel, Pennsylvania Historical and Museum Commission, Harrisburg, Pennsylvania; Beverly Walker, Frederic Remington Art Museum, Ogdensburg, New York; Gregory C. Schwarz, U. S. Department of the Interior, National Parks Service, Saint-Gaudens National Historic Site, Cornish, New Hampshire.

Finally, very special thanks to the employees who were involved in the gallery renovation and exhibit installation, especially Mike Ammons, Billy Beverly, Elijah Brown, Richard Parker, Marvin Smalls, John Strickland and Bill Weeks. Administrative staff Marvie Collins-Hughes and Sharon Herriott-Carr provided assistance, while volunteers Millie Doud, Amy Dickens and Pat Latstetter undertook valuable research.

Robin R. Salmon
Vice President & Curator of Sculpture
Brookgreen Gardens

Photography Credits

pg. 19: George Gray Barnard — Portrait by Anna Bilinska, The State Museum of Pennsylvania, Pennsylvania Historical & Museum Commission, Harrisburg, Pennsylvania

pgs. 24, 25, 29, 31, 34, 36, 37, 47, 57, 58: Henry Clews, Jr; Donald De Lue; Marshall Fredericks; Glenna Goodacre; Walker Hancock; Anna Hyatt Huntington; Carl Paul Jennewein; Carl Milles; Katharine Weems; A. A. Weinman — Brookgreen Garden Archives, Murrells Inlet, South Carolina

pgs. 20, 21, 23, 32, 50, 59: Paul Bartlett; Gutzon Borglum; Stirling Calder; Charles Grafly; Hiram Powers; Gertrude Whitney — Library of Congress, Washington, D. C.

pgs. 26, 44: Charlotte Dunwiddie; Isidore Margulies — National Sculpture Society, New York City

pgs. 28, 41, 51: James Earle Fraser; Frederick MacMonnies; Brenda Putnam — Peter A. Juley & Son Collection, National Museum of American Art, Smithsonian Institution, Washington, D. C.

pg. 30: Daniel Chester French — Chesterwood, a museum property of the National Trust for Historic Preservation, Stockbridge, Massachusetts

pg. 39: Gertrude Lathrop — Portrait by I. P. Lathrop, National Academy of Design, New York City

pg. 43: Paul Manship — National Portrait Gallery, Washington, D. C.

pg. 46: Richard McDermott Miller — courtesy of Richard McDermott Miller, New York City

pg. 49: Charles Parks — courtesy of Charles Parks Studio, Wilmington, Delaware

pg. 52: Frederic Remington — courtesy Frederic Remington Art Museum, Ogdensburg, New York

pg. 53: Augustus Saint-Gaudens — U. S. Department of the Interior, National Parks Service, Saint-Gaudens National Historic Site, Cornish, New Hampshire

pg. 55: Lorado Taft — Chicago Historical Society, Chicago, Illinois